Management Accounting in Hotel Groups

Paul Collier
University of Exeter

and

Alan Gregory
University of Exeter

The Chartered Institute of Management Accountants
63 Portland Place
N 4AB

Copyright © CIMA 1995

First published in 1995 by:

The Chartered Institute of Management Accountants

ISBN 1 874784 32 9

The publisher of this book considers that it is a worthwhile contribution to discussion, without necessarily sharing the views expressed, which are those of the authors.

No responsibility for loss occasioned to any person acting or refraining from action as a result of any material in this publication can be accepted by the authors or publisher.

Contents

Acknowledgements

The authors would like to thank the CIMA Research Foundation for funding the project.

Thanks are also due to the six senior personnel in the hotel groups whose management accounting systems are described in this report. Their assistance in patiently answering our questions and reading the case studies was much appreciated. We should also like to thank Howarth Consulting and Pannell Kerr Forster Associates for the information they contributed to this project.

Executive Summary

The research was conducted as part of an initiative by the Chartered Institute of Management Accountants to explore management accounting in the service sector. The hotel sector was chosen as an area for study, first because hotel groups are a key component of the vitally important tourist industry, and second because hotel groups combine property investment with the provision of a service.

The research looked at two main areas: (i) the provision of information for planning and control purposes; and (ii) decision-making. In the latter instance, the emphasis was on cost information for price determination, information and techniques to assist with investment decisions, and the use of strategic management accounting in the planning process and in taking decisions on marketing, finance and investment.

The approach adopted for addressing the research issues was to undertake case study research. Six companies which provided a mix of sizes, ownership and spread of operations were interviewed, and case studies which described their use of management accounting were prepared.

Strategic management accounting was widely used in the preparation of long-term plans, and in the monitoring by the accounting function of the cost structures and pricing policies of competitors. The importance of strategic management accounting reflects the open, relatively homogeneous nature of the industry, the ready availability of such data, and the high degree of competitiveness among the hotel groups in the market.

Costing systems, which were based on marginal costs with labour generally being treated as a fixed cost, focused on departmental performance. Overhead cost control reflected a separation of costs into controllable and uncontrollable costs categories and a focus on total wage costs. Despite the high fixed costs associated with the industry, none of the hotel groups interviewed used activity-based costing. The reasons given for the failure to apply this technique included the integrated nature of operations, staff flexibility and interchangeability, high margins and the fact that prices are market based. Pricing was a complex area, given the bundled nature of the services provided and the distinct market segments in a hotel. Prices were found to be driven almost entirely by market forces.

As might be anticipated, considerable time and effort were expended in the preparation of budgets which would typically be fixed iteratively, since the hotel general manager had local knowledge and head office had a better picture of general economic circumstances and the overall group performance target. In general, performance was based on performance against budget subject to meeting various service quality standards. However, there were considerable differences in the reward systems used, with a third of the cases having no bonus scheme for rewarding senior management.

The greatest variation in approach was in the area of investment appraisal, where a variety of techniques and combinations of techniques were used. Considerable emphasis was placed on the processes followed in estimating the occupancy percentages and average room rate, and strategic fit. As regards techniques, the more sophisticated approaches based around discounted cash flow methods tended to be used in hotel companies which were subsidiaries of non-hotel groups where a hands-on approach to management was not taken at the hotel company. By contrast, parent firms in the hotel and leisure sector, and those where the hotel company's head had a hands-on management style, tended to use more simplistic approaches to financial appraisal.

1
Introduction

Hotels were defined by the Hotels and Catering Economic Development Committee as 'an establishment of a permanent nature, of four or more bedrooms, offering bed and breakfast on a short-term contract and providing certain minimum standards'. The focus of this research is the use of management accounting information not in individual hotels, as this is well documented in studies like *Thornfield* (1991) or *Parkinson* (1993), but in the management of groups of hotels.

1.1 Reasons for the research

The research was conducted as part of an initiative by the Chartered Institute of Management Accountants to explore management accounting in the service sector,[1] an initiative which reflected the growing importance of this sector in terms of national income and employment.[2] The hotel sector was chosen as an area for study for three reasons. First, hotel groups have certain unusual characteristics as a business due to the dual nature of their activities involving property and management. Second, hotel groups are a key component of the vitally important tourist industry. Finally, there is an absence of research in this area.

---

1 Service industries comprise those included in sections 6–9 of the Standard Industrial Classification.
2 In terms of GDP at constant factor cost, the percentage of national income derived from the service sector rose from 51.7 per cent in 1981 to 69.0 per cent in 1990 (*UK National Accounts Blue Book*, CSO, 1991, Table 2.4), while between 1971 and 1990 the proportion of the total workforce in the service sector rose from 52.5 per cent to 69.7 per cent (CSO, Table 4.11; *Employment Gazette*, April 1991, p. 201).

Industry characteristics

- The industry is capital intensive – but in the long term the assets may reasonably be expected to hold their value and are not subject to obsolescence provided:
  (i) adequate funds are devoted to maintenance; *and*
  (ii) the earnings of the business are maintained.
- Asset values and management are inseparable – asset values depend on management's ability to generate profits.

An unusual feature of the industry is the existence of a specialised accounting body which is specific to the industry. The British Association of Hotel Accountants (BAHA) has over 1000 members, a regular newsletter (*BAHA Times*), runs conferences and training, and has a technical committee which produces statements of recommended practice on matters like the valuation of hotels (BAHA, 1993).

A past characteristic has been the existence of charismatic leaders in hotel groups: for example, Lord Forte at Forte plc, John Jarvis at Jarvis Hotels, John Bairstow at Queens Moat Houses plc, and Robert Peel at Mount Charlotte Hotels. Some of these entrepreneurs have had a keen following (although recent developments at Queens Moat Houses may have dampened enthusiasm), considerable influence on the management style of their companies and their philosophies, and may well have shaped their organisations' control systems.

Tourist industry

The tourist industry is one of the largest industries in the UK, providing both employment and a large contribution to invisible earnings. Hotels are a crucial part of this industry. Hotels are a diverse sector ranging from large hotel chains like Forte plc to a plethora of small independent units. At 31 March 1992 Hotel and Leisure companies comprised 2.5 per cent of the FT all share index in terms of market capitalisation, and at least five companies in the FTSE–100 index have substantial hotel interests. These figures ignore the fact that several major brewers and other companies outside this sector own hotel chains (although similarly not all companies in the Hotels and Leisure sector have major hotel interests). Further, in 1990 consumer expenditure on hotels and catering accounted for 7.5 per cent of all consumer expenditure.

Absence of research

Although there are a number of texts (see for example, *Everett* (1989), *Thornfield* (1991) or *Parkinson* (1993)) which cover management accounting within a hotel in some detail, there is no accounting literature on management accounting and its contribution to the management of groups of hotels.

1.2 Research objectives

It may be anticipated that the management of hotel groups would require the provision of information to assist with planning and control, and decision-making. The planning and control aspects would include the monitoring of performance against agreed targets set for individual hotels and their operating departments (rooms, food, beverages, leisure facilities, etc.), and the head office functions. Decision-making situations for which management accounting might be necessary might include the following:

- Pricing – cost information for price determination, and information on the relationship between price and demand;
- Investment decisions – information and analyses to assist with decisions on new builds, divestments, and extensions and refurbishments to existing hotels; and
- Strategy – the use of strategic management accounting in taking strategic decisions on marketing, finance, and investment.

The scope specifically excludes management accounting in individual hotels, which is well covered in texts such as *Thornfield* (1991) and *Parkinson* (1993).

1.3 Research method

The approach adopted for addressing the research issues was to undertake case study research. *Ryan et al.* (1992) identified five classes of case study: descriptive; illustrative; experimental; exploratory; and explanatory. The case study approach used in this research is firstly descriptive in that it documents the use of management accounting information in a number cases. However, it is hoped that the cases will permit exploration and explanation of the uses of management accounting information which are discovered. Thus, as well as reporting management accounting practices, there will be an attempt to generate hypotheses about the reasons for them, and explain them by reference to theory.

Case study research by its nature raises questions about its validity and the extent to which generalisations can be drawn from the results. As regards the validity of the case study approach, its merits have been well established by a number of authors (e.g. *Diesing* (1972) or *Mohr* (1985)). For example, Mohr argues that, although a case study has little statistical validity, it is marked by a depth or richness of detail and the ability to obtain insights into how the perceptions of interviewees have influenced the shape and use of management accounting information. Given this, it is not surprising that case study approaches have found support and been applied in numerous research projects (e.g. *Kaplan* (1984, 1986); *Rickwood et al.* (1987); *Davis et al.* (1991); and *Holland* (1993)). Generalisability, as discussed by *Scapens* (1990), was not the main objective of the research; rather, the case study was viewed as a means of discovering what was happening in practice in a limited number of organisations and to assist in the development of hypotheses which might explain the management accounting systems which were found. However, in interpreting the results it must be remembered that although our cases represent a significant portion of the 22 hotel groups which fell within our selection criteria, they are not necessarily representative, due, for example, to difficulties in gaining access to hotel groups which were experiencing financial difficulties. Thus, it is possible that the cases are biased towards companies with best practice on the assumption that a link exists between good management accounting practices and financial success. Alternatively, the willingness of some finance directors to divert scarce resources in co-operating with the research may reflect a strong personal interest in the promotion of management accounting in the industry.

Selection of case study subjects

The population was identified from the *UK Hotel Groups Directory 1992/93* (*Harrison and Johnson* (1992)), which details the holding companies of UK hotel groups.

In order to limit the size of the population, a minimum turnover of £25 million per annum was set. The companies approached were selected on the basis of obtaining a mix of the following three characteristics:

(i) status – a mix of public limited companies, limited companies (private companies), and subsidiaries with examples of UK and foreign ownership;

(ii) size – cases which varied from groups of under 20 hotels to over 100 hotels, as control systems in particular may well be different depending on the number of units being controlled; and

(iii) spread of operations – a mix of groups that operated both nationally and internationally.

Ten hotel groups were identified and their finance director contacted by letter. Six hotel groups responded positively. An analysis of the companies in terms of the main selection criteria is given in Table 1.1.

Table 1.1 Summary of the main characteristics of the case study companies

Reference	Status	Size based on no. of hotels*	Spread
A	UK-based limited company	Medium	UK
B	UK-based plc	Large	International
C	Subsidiary of overseas company	Small	International
D	Subsidiary of overseas company	Large	UK
E	Subsidiary of UK plc	Medium	UK
F	Subsidiary of UK plc	Small	UK

*	Small:	up to 25 hotels
	Medium:	25 – 75 hotels
	Large:	over 75 hotels

The only deficiency in the spread of cases across the criteria was that only one public limited company which specialised in hotels was prepared to grant an interview. Two additional public limited companies beyond the three originally approached were written to but without success. One obvious explanation for this lack of success was the financial difficulties that a number of listed hotel groups were experiencing over the period of the research. The most widely publicised problems were with Queens Moat Houses plc, but a number of smaller groups were also in severe difficulties and naturally may not have viewed discussing control systems as a priority or even desirable, given the belief that poor control systems might have contributed to the difficulties experienced by Queens Moat Houses plc.

Procedure

The procedure followed in all cases was to send interviewees an *aide-mémoire* listing areas of interest and use this document as a base for the discussions. After the interview, a case study would be written up and a copy sent to the interviewee for agreement/amendment. A further follow-up interview was held, where necessary, to clarify relevant issues. The details of approaches to management accounting in this research are based on the agreed narratives.

1.4 Background information on the case study companies

For reasons of confidentiality, none of the case study companies are named. For referencing them in the text, the cases were assigned a letter A–F in chronological order based on when the first visit occurred. To enable a better understanding of each case study, a more detailed background follows.

Company A (Interviewee – group management accountant)

The subject of the case study is a private company which was formed recently for the buyout of a hotel chain. The company currently owns and manages a chain of under 50 UK hotels. The size of hotels and their characters vary widely, with the smallest hotel having only around twenty bedrooms and the largest over 200 bedrooms. The board of directors has a chairman and chief executive and deputy chief executive who between them receive reports from directors responsible for six functional areas: operations of hotels (north); operations of hotels (south); sales and marketing; property; human resources; and finance. These head office support functions are run by a staff of around 40.

The finance function is the responsibility of a financial controller and is split into financial accounting and management accounting departments. The former is responsible for 'balance sheet' areas such as cash management, taxation and funding, while the latter focuses on 'profit and loss account' matters, for example the planning cycle and performance evaluation. The year is divided for management accounting purposes into 13 periods of 4 weeks each. In the 4-week period the management accounts department spends weeks 1 and 2 producing the management accounts, week 3 at hotels assisting them with problems, and week 4 preparing board papers. The hotel management teams vary widely in number and expertise depending on the size of the hotel.

The management style is fairly decentralised, with individual hotel managers being given considerable freedom in the running of the hotels subject to meeting agreed profit targets and obtaining approval for major capital projects. The adherence to target profit levels is reinforced by a bonus scheme for senior hotel management based upon attainment of at least 95 per cent of the target profit. However, there are attempts to standardise in certain areas – for example, the standard of equipment in rooms, and wine lists.

The current structure of operations is hierarchical with performance related to revenue less direct costs, other costs such as payroll being treated as fixed costs. This approach is currently under review. It is proposed that a business (profit) centre basis is adopted and the bonus scheme widened to include business centre managers. The business centres would include conferences, leisure, banqueting, restaurant and others, with the general manager 'liberated' to promote the hotel and 'troubleshoot'. The cost information for the new system would be at a direct cost level with payroll costs obtained from the wages sheets. The revised organisation structure has the effect of freeing the hotel general manager to enable him to develop the business.

The head office offers a range of services to hotels, including a central reservation service, the planning of a number of promotions including special packages and management expertise and advice to hotels in areas like beverages and food. Each hotel has its own bank account but the balances are consolidated daily into a group bank account.

As might be expected with a buyout, the company has substantial borrowings and is restricted by a number of loan covenants. As a result, cash generation is a highly significant objective as is remaining within covenant targets. A stock exchange floatation is a medium-term objective.

Company B (Interviewee – finance director)

The subject of the case study is a subsidiary of a major public company in the hotel and leisure industry. The company currently manages a chain of over 200 UK hotels and over 50 overseas hotels, principally in Europe. In general the hotels managed are wholly owned, although in Europe a small number are subject to management contracts. The size of hotels and their characters vary widely, but like hotels are grouped into strategic business units (SBUs) which manage the brand of the hotels in the grouping. The board of directors of the company is headed by a managing director who receives reports from directors responsible for the following five functional areas: marketing; property; human resources; operations; and finance. These head office support functions are run by a staff of over 600 of whom over half are in the worldwide marketing function. For management accounting and reporting purposes, the year is divided into monthly periods based on calender months.

The management style is centralised and the group structure is hierarchical, with each of the standard business units having a team of around six (managing director, commercial director, sales and marketing director, and regional directors) who report to the operations director on the main board and manage the hotels within the brand grouping. Individual hotels are managed by a general manager who is responsible for maintaining standards, developing local business, and cost control. Hotel general managers are given incentives based on cash-generation targets. The targets are varied from time to time to focus upon different aspects of the business according to current areas of concern, for example catering margins.

Individual hotels do not have specialist staff in accounting, human resources and other areas; rather, there are administrative support groups which provide specialist services to clusters of hotels. The head office offers a range of services to hotels, including a central reservation service, the obtaining of business through a number of promotions including special packages, and management expertise and advice to hotels. Hotels do not have their own bank accounts and all purchasing and bank payments and receipts are dealt with through head office. The costs of the administrative support groups are charged to hotels but hotels are not generally charged for head office services, although such costs may be allocated to the brands. The exceptions to this principle are standard levies on budgeted turnover of hotels for sales and marketing, personnel management including training, and maintenance.

Company C (Interviewee – finance director)

The subject of the case study is a hotel group owned by an overseas company. The hotel group manages approximately 20 hotels of which a third are overseas, mainly in Europe. Although the majority of hotels are wholly owned, the hotel group also has hotels where the company holds a majority or minority equity stake and runs them under a management contract or even no equity stake and just a management contract. A typical management contract is for 20–25 years with an option for a further 10 years. The hotels vary in size from around 100 to almost 1000 bedrooms. The company is given considerable autonomy in its management of the hotels in the group. Control is exercised by the parent through membership of the company board, approval of significant capital expenditure, and internal audit. The board of the company is composed of four parent company directors plus the chief executive and finance director from the hotel group. The board meets monthly to review performance of the group and individual hotels against budget, examine future strategies and formulate plans.

The company has a decentralised approach to managing the individual hotels in the group. This decentralised approach is reflected in the small complement at head office, where under 25 staff are involved in the day-to-day supervision of the hotels. The chief executive, who has an operations background and is in everyday control of the group, is reported to by the following functional areas: development; sales and marketing; technical services; operations; finance; and human resources. The sales and marketing director is responsible for formulating and executing the group marketing strategy, which is paid for by a single rate fixed percentage levy on the budgeted turnover of each of the hotels. The strategy includes the marketing and pricing of weekend packages and other promotions. Hotels are expected to undertake local promotions but have complete autonomy in their targeting and approach. The human resources director deals with the statutory and other legal matters related to the employees in the group, provides assistance and advice to human resource managers at hotels, and is responsible for senior appointments at head office and the hotels. The developments director is responsible for initiating new projects and negotiations with entrepreneurs or developers with propositions for equity or management contract involvement. The company employs outside advisers to assist with the evaluation of major investments. The finance director is reported to by a group financial controller, who is responsible for individual hotel budgeting and monthly reporting, and a corporate financial controller, who is responsible for the consolidated entity.

Company D (Interviewee – senior director)

The subject of this case study is a large company which is a subsidiary of a foreign-owned multinational. The company specialises in the hotel trade and is operated with a considerable degree of autonomy from the parent. The company manages a portfolio of over 100 hotels, the majority of which are owned although a limited number are on management contracts. The company is organised partially on a branded basis, but mostly on a geographical basis for the largest brand. The management style is highly centralised, with the managing director taking a hands-on approach to running the firm.

Formal management accounting systems do not figure strongly in either decision-making or performance evaluation, although budgets are used as a control and planning tool. No bonuses are paid for good performance, neither are managers dismissed for failing to meet budgets.

The company has seen considerable expansion. New hotel investment analyses give heavy weight to strategic considerations; location is seen as being of fundamental importance, but the judgement of the managing director and his co-director are based mainly on 'feel' and their experience in the industry. All new hotel investments have been acquisitions of existing hotels either as individual purchases or as portfolio acquisitions. The only 'new build' done by the company was the completion of a construction project following one of these takeovers. A major consideration of all hotel acquisitions when the company had been independent was the non-dilution of earnings per share in the year following acquisition, although in one case a 3–5 year view was taken on this issue.

The head office of the company consists of around 150 staff and the operation is seen as being 'pared to the bone', with only one qualified accountant being employed. The head office operations cover the regional management, accounting and finance, sales and marketing, and personnel, although sales and marketing is dominant in terms of the staff employed. The company's customer base includes around 30 per cent tour company income, with the balance being largely corporate and individual clients. Tour guests are seen as useful because they fill the hotels over the weekend period. Leisure breaks also help business in this respect. Restaurants are seen as being a support service to guests, so that the objective is cost recovery (although the definition of cost here includes an informally assessed opportunity cost of the space utilised by the restaurant).

Company E (Interviewee – finance director)

The subject of the case study is a wholly-owned subsidiary of a listed company operating in the UK brewing industry. The company's hotel portfolio originates partly from organic growth, and partly from acquisitions. It consists of under 30 hotels, covering a range of sizes and star ratings; some of these are rented, some are owned. No management contracts are undertaken, save for one hotel which is still owned by the parent. All general ledger, purchase ledger and cash book accounting is carried out at head office. Each hotel keeps its own debtors ledger and budgets are prepared at this level, with each hotel having a financial controller. Hotels are linked to head office by a computer network which allows them to order and buy autonomously, but payment and paperwork is dealt with centrally. All marketing was carried out by a small head office team, but hotels have recently been allowed to carry out supplementary local marketing. Leisure brochures, hotel directories and price lists are all produced centrally in order to create uniformity of style. The organisation consists of five departments: sales and marketing; personnel and training; accounting and administration; estates; and operations. The latter department is further broken down between two regional managers and a leisure operations manager.

In terms of the management accounting system, the budgets (3-year and 1-year) are central to the planning and control process. The system appears to show a heavily participative style, with the emphasis on budgets as forecasts rather than targets; hotel general managers were expected to be 'realistic but positive' in their forecasting. In general, the style of management accounting was described as not bounded by rules and manuals. It is regarded as an advantage that the company is small enough for the chief accountant to know the individual hotel managers. There is also a culture of openness in the exchange of ideas with other hotel accountants, both through personal contact and through BAHA.

The hotels subsidiary has its own balance sheet, and funds all capital expenditure through an overdraft from the parent. Similarly, it is allowed to retain all proceeds from disposals. A key feature of the company's strategy is revenue maximisation; to this end, yield management systems have been employed (based upon those used by airlines) and an airline-style on-line central reservations system (CRS) is employed. This system is compatible with all the major on-line booking systems used by travel agents.

Company F (Interviewee – finance director)

The subject of the case study is a division of a public listed company which operates in the food, drinks and accommodation sectors. The hotel division currently owns and manages fewer than ten hotels which range in size from around 50 to almost 200 rooms. The hotels are all of around three- to four-star standard and are situated in the UK. No management contracts are undertaken.

The hotels are managed from a small head office of just over 20 staff. The board consists of a managing director, finance director, personnel director and operations director. The head office functions cover finance and management accounting, personnel, marketing, and operations, including maintenance and new developments.

Contracts for the supply of the majority of food and drink, and some other services, are negotiated centrally. Some hotels have their own bank accounts, but all accounts are consolidated at division level and treasury management functions are run by the group treasury function. For capital expenditure, hotels are funded by the division and the division obtains its funds from the group. Head office imposes a levy based upon budgeted sales to cover training and marketing costs. These levies ensure that adequate funds are devoted to key areas. The head office marketing effort focuses on brand development but local advertising will be paid for by the centre if it is agreed in advance and general managers may undertake any advertising if they are prepared to pay for it locally.

1.5 *Structure of the research report*

Chapter 2 examines the use made of strategic management accounting by hotel groups. It identifies two main areas for strategic management accounting information, first, in the preparation of long-term plans, and second, in the monitoring by the accounting function (at least to some degree) of the cost structures and pricing policies of competitors. The considerable involvement of accounting functions in strategic management accounting is consistent with the open, relatively homogeneous nature of the industry, the ready availability of such data, and the high degree of competitiveness among the hotel groups in the market.

Chapter 3 covers the provision of management accounting information for costing and pricing. The costing systems were based on marginal costs, with labour generally being treated as a fixed cost. Another consistent characteristic of the accounting system was a departmental approach to the measurement of performance. Overhead cost control reflected a separation of costs into controllable and uncontrollable costs categories and a focus on wage costs. Pricing was a complex area, given the bundled nature of the services provided and the distinct market segments in a hotel. Prices were found to be driven almost entirely by market forces and management accounting was restricted to limited areas like menu determination.

Chapter 4 considers the use of budgets. The budgeting process, both annual and in the longer term, was the major area in which time and effort was expended by management accountants.

Typically, budgets were fixed iteratively. Head office would supply the individual hotels with economic and marketing data and a standard pro forma for completion. Several meetings between the hotel general manager and senior management would take place before a final version was agreed. Variance analysis was done on a line-by-line basis, and in general budgets were not flexed, although most hotel groups undertook forecasts of the outcome for a period forward using actuals as a starting-point.

Chapter 5 demonstrates considerable commonality in performance evaluation both in financial and non-financial terms. In general, performance was based on performance against budget subject to meeting various service quality standards. However, there were considerable differences in the reward systems used, with a third of the cases having no bonus scheme for rewarding senior management.

The final area of discussion was investment appraisal, which is dealt with in Chapter 6. Discussions included the process followed in estimating cash flows and the techniques used. The situation in hotel groups is unusual in that decisions are classifiable into homogeneous groups, such as new builds, acquisitions, extensions, and refurbishments. It might be anticipated that there would be a commonality of approach, but a wide range of techniques was employed with perhaps the greatest emphasis being on market forecasts of occupancy levels and average room rates.

2
The Use of Strategic Management Accounting

2.1 Introduction

The interviewees were asked whether strategic management accounting was employed. The working definition used was obtained from CIMA (1982), which describes strategic management accounting as 'The provision and analysis of management accounting data relating to a business strategy: particularly the relative levels and trends in real costs and prices, volumes, market share, cash flow and the demands on a firm's total resources.' The definition was chosen in preference to the alternatives like the one provided by Bromwich,[1] because it recognises that data relevant to business strategy may well be non-financial. Discussions at the case study companies revealed that interviewees identified two main strategic management accounting areas: first, the provision of information that assisted in the development of long-term strategic plans; and second, monitoring the market, competitors' price structures, and competitors' costs.

2.2 Strategic planning

Strategic planning was formalised through the preparation of long-term budgets in all the case study companies except D. In company D, the tight personal control exercised by the managing director resulted in the strategy of the hotel group being developed by the managing director in liaison with the parent company. The period covered by the long-term budgets varied, but all were

---

1 Bromwich (1990) defined strategic management accounting as 'The provision and analysis of financial information on the firm's product markets and competitors' costs and cost structures and the monitoring of the enterprise's strategies and those of competitors in these markets over a number of periods.'

updated annually. In case studies A, B and C the planning exercise looked five years forward, whereas in cases E and F the process was limited to three years forward. In all cases the starting-point was the budget for the following year. The scope of all the long-term budgets was limited to the balance sheet, profit and loss account, and cash flow statement. In the case of A, the planning system was based around a spreadsheet model developed at the time of the buyout by external consultants. In the other four case studies, the long-term budgets were developed from the existing budget system. Case E was typical of the level of detail. At hotel level the most important elements were occupancy percentage multiplied by average room rate to give room yield. Food and bars contribution is brought in through a given percentage margin, and expenses are analysed into wages in salaries and other overheads with a fixed adjustment made for rents. In all cases it was pointed out that forecasts beyond one year forward are inevitably increasingly subjective and dependent on various assumptions. However, it was inevitable that a longer time-horizon had to be taken as one year forward is insufficient for planning the structure and funding of the business.

The stated objectives of the long-term budgets were to provide a framework within which

(a) management could consider the future and explore the effect of alternative strategies;
(b) provide an indication of the future shape of the business; *and*
(c) highlight the future financial structure of the group and identify and schedule future financing requirements.

However, the emphasis varied with the situation of the individual company. Thus in A, the exercise was specifically aimed at providing information in a form suitable for presentation to the financing institutions. This situation is in part explained by the anticipated low level of acquisition and disposal activity in the medium term. In contrast, in case study E (which had a more active approach to acquisitions and disposals), although the long-term budget and its review with head office were key to planning the cash requirements and funding of the company by the parent, it was also integral to the evaluation of strategic alternatives. In C, where there was a move to expand through management contracts and joint ventures as well as acquisitions, the long-term budgets focused on the impact of changes in the mix of hotels and the mix of ownership schemes. The mix of hotels will change as planned developments come on stream. The assumption was that new hotels will take time to reach a steady earning position and that at any point in time the group will consist of a portfolio of hotels in varying states of maturity. The mix of ownership schemes reflects possible new investments, joint ownership schemes and new management contracts that might come on stream over the period to provide a second dimension to the portfolio. The principle objective of long-term plans is to consider the impact of different maturity and ownership mixes and to plan finance requirements which reflect the chosen mix in conjunction with the parent.

At Company F, the input by the accounting function into the development of strategic plans included a formal SWOT analysis exercise.[2] The exercise plotted the hotel group's 'competitive capabilities' against 'business sector attractiveness'. A range of business sectors were examined (for example food, drink, accommodation, and leisure) and the position of the company compared with competitors was determined by using a range of measurable variables collected by in-house staff and external consultants. The exercise was deemed useful but deficient in so far as it did not take account of the relative costs of changing competitive position in the various business sectors.

2.3 *Monitoring the market, competitors' price structures and competitors' costs*

Bromwich (1990) stressed that there is a need for accountants to consider the cost structure not only of their own firm but of all enterprises in the relevant market and of potential entrants, and that cost cannot be considered in isolation from demand factors. This aspect of strategic management accounting relies on the availability of relevant information. The hotel sector meets these requirements due to the open nature of the industry and the availability of price and some cost data.

Several of the interviewees described the industry as being fairly open, especially for the interchange of ideas on different

---

2 See Bhattacharya (1988) for a discussion of the role of the management accountant in SWOT analysis.

approaches to solving common problems like automated booking systems, valuation practices and yield management systems. The common forum for such discussions is the British Association of Hotel Accountants (BAHA), which has over a thousand members; a number of the interviewees, especially those who had spent the majority of their working life in the industry, were members.

The nature of the industry makes it difficult for companies to be secretive about such matters as prices or costs. Rack rates and other standard terms are publicised, and it is possible to pose as a customer to ascertain discounts off the published rates. On the cost side, major components of costs may be determined with a degree of accuracy – for example, the valuation of hotels, site costs and building costs can be monitored and rateable values are publicly available.

As with strategic planning, major consultants specialising in the field offered services which were relevant to strategic management accounting. For example, Howarth Consulting produce an annual survey of hotels from throughout the UK with detailed summaries that act as a basis for interfirm comparison. The 1992 *Statistical Report* was based on returns from 293 hotels and included data analysed across four regions (London; Provinces; Scotland; and Wales) and across a variety of average room rates. The terminology used and accounts titles conformed to the *Uniform System of Accounts for Hotels*.

The reports covered:

- Average Room Occupancy and Rates – average annual room occupancy; average number of guests per room; average daily room rate; and four categories based on average rate per guest night.
- Market Information – guest analysis by country; percentage of repeat business; percentage of guests with advance reservations; and account settlement method.
- Operational Data – percentage composition of sales split by rooms, food, beverage, and other; cost of sales data; gross operating profit; and employee statistics.
- Revenue per Guest Night – rooms; telephone and telex; minor operating departments; and rental and other income.
- Payroll and Other Expenses – both in terms of amount per available room and percentage of total revenue with a split across rooms, food and beverages, administrative and general, marketing,

and property operations and maintenance.
- Food and Beverage Statistics – analysed by facility, percentage of total food sales, amount per seat, and per cover.
- Departmental Revenues and Expenses – in total and analysed by room across rooms, food, beverage, telephone, minor operating departments, and rental and other income.

Table 2.1 (overleaf) gives an example of the information available. The table shows high-level operational data which is analysed in more detail in subsequent reports.

In this environment it is not surprising that in all but two of the case studies (A and F), the accounting function monitored to some degree the cost structures and pricing policies of competitors. In A, where there was no strategic management accounting within the accounting function, competitor price review and market data assessment was the responsibility of the marketing function. In the case of F, although the accounting function took an interest in competitors' actions, no detailed studies were undertaken using published accounts, brokers' reports, analysts' reports or other data sources. Again, the marketing function had responsibility for monitoring market conditions and the actions of competitors. The absence of any strategic management accounting in these cases is perhaps explained by special circumstances. In both cases, the groupings had only been recently formed and were focusing inwards on developing a market niche rather than being concerned with the actions of competitors.

In another two case studies strategic management accounting was carried out irregularly by the accounting function. In D, although no formal analysis was made of competitors' cost structures, a keen interest was taken in competitors' actions. Further, the performance of the company against competitors was compared regularly at a return on sales level, and information was gleaned from brokers' reports. However, in line with the less formalised control approach in this company, reliance was principally placed on senior managements' experience in the hotel industry and the steps they take to keep in touch with their hotel general managers. The accounting function in case study E followed up their competitors' actions through an examination of published accounts, brokers' reports and analysts' reports.

The most wide-ranging exercises in strategic accounting were

Table 2.1 Hotel strategic operational data

	UK		London		Provinces		Scotland	
	1991	1990	1991	1990	1991	1990	1991	1990
PERCENTAGE COMPOSITION OF SALES	%	%	%	%	%	%	%	%
Rooms	47.9	47.4	61.6	61.7	45.5	44.1	44.8	45.7
Food	31.7	32.0	21.6	21.4	33.6	34.4	34.0	34.1
Beverage	13.5	14.3	8.5	8.7	14.3	15.7	15.3	14.3
Minor operating departments	6.1	4.5	7.2	7.0	5.8	3.9	5.1	4.9
Rental and other income	0.8	1.7	1.1	1.2	0.8	2.0	0.8	1.1
	100.0	100.0	100.0	100.0	100.0	100.0	100.0	100.0
COST OF SALES AS A PERCENTAGE OF DEPARTMENTAL REVENUE	%	%	%	%	%	%	%	%
Food	35.2	35.0	34.0	34.6	36.2	35.2	33.3	34.2
Beverage	33.6	33.9	29.3	32.1	34.3	34.2	35.5	35.6
DEPARTMENTAL OPERATING PROFIT AS A PERCENTAGE OF DEPARTMENTAL REVENUE	%	%	%	%	%	%	%	%
Rooms	69.9	71.0	71.9	73.0	69.4	70.4	68.3	69.8
Food and beverage	27.8	28.5	19.1	20.0	29.8	30.0	28.4	31.0
GROSS OPERATING PROFIT AS PERCENTAGE OF TOTAL SALES	29.4	32.4	33.9	37.3	32.8	31.0	27.8	32.4
EMPLOYEE STATISTICS								
Employees per available room	0.95	1.11	0.84	1.24	0.95	0.97	1.24	1.15
Sales per employee (£)	31,669	28,334	43,749	43,366	27,046	23,727	21,239	20,796
Cost per employee (£)	10,182	8,455	13,853	12,953	8,815	7,198	7,256	6,041
Payroll and related expenses as a percentage of total sales	31.2	29.0	30.6	27.4	34.8	29.5	31.6	29.2
Productivity index (total sales divided by payroll & related expenses)	3.3	3.6	3.4	3.8	3.3	3.5	3.2	3.5

Note: all figures are means, i.e. the simple arithmetic average

Reproduced with permission of Howarth Consulting

found in B and C. Company B regularly undertook *ad hoc* strategic management accounting exercises. The exercises focused on competitor performance and market data assessment. At one level, statistical information was obtained from the published accounts and related brokers' reports of major competitors and their performance compared with the company. In particular, performance was compared on a monthly basis with another group which was felt to be the closest in business areas to the company. The company regularly tracks its performance against market surveys prepared by consultants specialising in the industry. In C, the assessment of position relative to competitors was undertaken through an examination of published accounts and the use of some base data on rooms which was exchanged with other hotel chains in a similar class of business. This 'interfirm comparison' type of exercise enables a crude comparison of room performance against competitors to be compared at a regional level.

One common result of strategic management accounting activity was suspicion about the performance of Queens Moat Houses plc, which was shown to be the clear market leader in the sector. Generally, the view was that the results were highly suspicious and 'too good to be true'. One case study company was sufficiently interested to commission a consultants' report on the company to identify how it produced the results. However, none of the companies were able to fully understand the processes that had led to the apparently excellent results revealed in the published report and accounts.

2.4 Summary

The findings, which are summarised in Table 2.2, show that the accounting function in hotel groups has considerable involvement in strategic management accounting. The least use of strategic management accounting was made by D, a company where formal management accounting systems did not feature strongly either in decision-making or performance evaluation.

The prevalence of strategic management accounting is consistent with the open and relatively homogeneous nature of the industry and the high degree of competitiveness among the hotel groups in the market.

Table 2.2 Summary of the uses of strategic management accounting

Company	Development of long-term strategic plans	Time horizon (years)	Monitor competitors' price structure and costs
A	Yes	5	No
B	Yes	5	Yes
C	Yes	5	Yes
D	No	n/a	Irregular
E	Yes	3	Irregular
F	Yes	3	No

3

Management Accounting Information for Costing and Pricing

3.1 Costing information

As has been already observed, hotels are fairly homogeneous business entities and thus it is unremarkable that attempts have been made to standardise and formalise hotel accounting practice. In the USA, the *Uniform System of Accounts for Hotels* was formally adopted by the American Hotel Association in 1926, and currently it is a revised edition of this that is widely used in the USA (Hotel Association of New York City, 1986). The UK equivalent was provided by the Hotel and Catering Economic Development Council which drew up *A Standard System of Hotel Accounting* (HMSO, 1969). The UK approach appears to have used the US system as a guide since both systems split the hotel into operating revenue-earning departments and services departments or overhead groupings. The operating statements show:

  (i) revenue analysed by major operating department;
  (ii) cost of sales related to each major operating department;
  (iii) payroll and other costs analysed for each major operating department;
  (iv) operating profits for each department and total operating profits;
  (v) costs of service departments or overhead groupings to give total overhead costs;
  (vi) profit before management fees and charges, being total departmental operating profit less total overhead costs;
  (vii) management fees, rent, rates and insurance to give net operating profit; and
  (viii) depreciation and interest which give rise to net profit before taxation.

In practice, the management accounting and costing systems for the hotels managed by the groups approximated to a marginal cost approach for each department with the assumption that labour was fixed. In practice, it was recognised that labour was probably a semi-variable cost and that the fixed-cost assumption was a simplification. However, the approach was rationalised on two grounds: first, that the benefits of a detailed analysis for decision-making were not deemed worthwhile in an environment where pricing was largely market based; and second, on the grounds that labour flexibility makes the allocation of labour to income streams extremely difficult. Another example of the practical approach to devising a costing system was the level of detail applied in identifying the variable costs for different departments. In all the case studies but one, the gross profit on rooms and leisure facilities was 100 per cent of revenue, while in the case of food and beverages it was revenue less the direct costs (materials) of food and beverages. From the gross operating profit was deducted direct wages (usually analysed by department) and direct expenses (similarly analysed) to arrive at what was referred to variously as 'total gross operating profit', 'gross departmental profit', 'total departmental contribution' and 'departmental profit'.

The findings are consistent with the observations of *Fitzgerald et al.* (1990), who noted that cost traceability would only be moderate in service shop environments, and that costs should be related to the functional activities of the business (e.g. rooms, food and beverages). It could also be argued that this revenue less direct material costs is analogous to throughput accounting with the hotel as a factory. This may not be wholly far-fetched, as one finance director referred to a hotel as 'a factory processing customers', nor is the use of throughput accounting inappropriate as there are parallels in cost structure with the modern factory. *Galloway and Waldron* (1988) argued that throughput accounting recognised the fact that, in a factory, the entire costs excluding material consumed is fixed in the short term and that therefore the focus of the systems must be on maximising the throughput defined as revenue less direct material costs. This is a process akin to the revenue-maximising objective expressed by the hotel groups interviewed.

The approach of focusing on contribution and gross profit at a departmental level was rationalised on the grounds that it assists with the aim of maximising the yield from the facilities. However, it does not readily permit break-even analysis due to the complicated cost and sales structure. In particular, the identification of the critical break-even occupancy percentage, which would be of considerable interest to senior management, has proved elusive. Recently, *Wijeysinghe* (1993) demonstrated an approach to calculating the break-even occupancy percentage by a number of restrictive assumptions, but only one of the hotel groups visited (B) used such an approach. Despite the high fixed costs associated with the industry, none of the hotel groups interviewed used activity-based costing. Reasons for this included the integrated nature of the activities, the high margins, and the market-based nature of pricing. On theoretical grounds, the absence of activity-based costing may be explained by the observations of *Bromwich and Bhimani* (1989) that decisions drive overhead costs and that most hotel costs derive from the decision to run a hotel of a certain capacity. However, the finding is at variance with *Fitzgerald et al.* (1990) who suggested that activity-based costing was likely to be especially useful in service shops, although it was conceded that its cost might outweigh its benefits.

The costing system adopted is well illustrated by the layout of the operating statements of individual hotels. There were a number of different presentations of these fundamental relationships which place different emphases on hotel performance.

At company B, as shown in Table 3.1, the 'contribution' was not specifically identified and the focus was on total gross operating profit. The gross operating profit was defined as sales less total cost of sales, total direct wages, and direct expenses. The gross operating profit was analysed between rooms, catering, and other, but the cost of sales, total direct wages, and direct expenses were not. Management here as at other hotels emphasised the importance of clearly identifying direct wage costs, as these costs were perceived as a major area for cost control. Expenses not directly attributable to activities (like general and administrative, sales and marketing, property costs, maintenance, and depreciation) were deducted from the gross operating profit to arrive at hotel profit contribution, against which is set any bonus to give hotel profit.

Table 3.1 The format of the operating statement in case study B

SALES
Rooms
Catering
Other
TOTAL SALES
Total cost of sales
Total direct wages
Direct expenses
GROSS OPERATING PROFIT
Rooms
Catering
Other
TOTAL GROSS OPERATING PROFIT
Expenses
General and administrative
Sales and marketing
Property costs
Maintenance
Depreciation
HOTEL PROFIT CONTRIBUTION
Bonus
HOTEL PROFIT

In other cases, the level of departmental analysis of cost was greater. Thus, in E, the gross profit on rooms and leisure facilities was 100 per cent of revenue, while in the case of food and beverages it was revenue less the direct material costs of food and beverages. From the gross profit (contribution) was deducted the costs of the departments to give the departmental contribution (really gross profit) against which was set the general overheads of the hotel (e.g. wages of the general manager and financial controller, staff wages, transport costs, maintenance, repairs and renewals, and depreciation) to arrive at a net profit before any rent. In F a similar approach was followed, but the labour and other non-administrative costs were allocated to departments in order to identify departmental net profits from which were subtracted administrative costs classified into controllable and non-controllable expenses.

In D a similar format was adopted, with gross profits being determined for rooms, food, liquor, tobacco and sundries. However, only wage costs analysed by the above areas were deducted to give the 'net margin' from which were deducted all expenses whether fixed or variable. The case was also unusual in that 40 categories of operating expense were identified, including flowers, paper squares, staff recruitment, and complaints. The failure to analyse direct costs to revenue lines was justified on the grounds that the variable element of costs was low and no useful data would be gained. The detailed analysis of expenses was seen as being an important means for controlling hotel managers. The net margin less operating expenses was called the profit before repairs and renewals, and from this was deducted repairs and renewals, bad debts, and depreciation to give the hotel net profit. Management accounting systems in A also equated with this approach, as potentially allocatable items like payroll costs, rates, and laundry were all treated as general unallocated overheads. However, the level of analysis was more detailed. For example, revenue from rooms was analysed for anticipated volume and average rate across rack (full) rates, business house rates, commercial rates, conference, group travel, leisure breaks and contract/tactical (business of a sizeable nature which occurs regularly). There were plans to adapt the system in the future when the business structure changes to identify business centres. The business centres will have overhead costs allocated to them: for example, payroll will be allocated to the centres, using time sheets. This revised approach mirrors that shown in Table 3.2, which was used by C.

The costing system at C most clearly identified departmental performance, with the revenues and variable costs for each department (rooms, food and beverage, communications, and other income) being matched in arriving at gross profit (contribution) from which was deducted fixed overheads. The analysis of costs into fixed and variable (cost per room sold) categories was fairly detailed: for example, the rooms department costs that vary with room occupancy levels and are therefore classified as variable costs include laundry, cleaning, and linen, etc. Other expenses which did not vary with the number of rooms sold (fixed costs such as TV licences, equipment rental, etc.) were offset against the gross departmental profit to provide a gross operating profit. The gross operating profit, which represented the profit less controllable costs, was reduced by uncontrollable costs such as the management fee and property taxes, to derive the net profit before interest and tax.

Table 3.2 The format of the operating statement in case study C

ROOMS DEPARTMENT
Sales
Payroll and related expenses
Other direct expenses

Department profit

FOOD AND BEVERAGE DEPARTMENT
Sales
Public room hire
Cost of sales
Payroll and related expenses
Other direct expenses

Department profit

COMMUNICATIONS
Sales
Cost of sales
Payroll and related expenses
Other direct expenses

Department profit

OTHER INCOME
Sales
Cost of sales
Payroll and related expenses
Other direct expenses

Department profit

GROSS DEPARTMENTAL PROFIT

UNDISTRIBUTED EXPENSES AND PAY
Administrative and general
Advertising and promotion
Energy
Repairs and maintenance

Total undistributed expenses

GROSS OPERATING PROFIT
Management fee
Property taxes
Insurance depreciation/amortisation
Rent
Total fixed costs

NET PROFIT BEFORE INTEREST AND TAX
Net interest

NET PROFIT BEFORE TAX

Revenues were analysed by market centres. A 'market centre' is a line of business; these consist of classifications such as rack rate, corporate–national (agreements negotiated by head office), corporate–local (agreements negotiated locally), and conference.

In the case studies, there was generally little emphasis given to standard costs beyond menu costing. In general, the management accounting system reported actual results in £'000s on a monthly basis. The actual figures were both for the month and the year to date, and comparisons with the budget and last year were made in two ways: first, by disclosing the budget position and last year's results for the month and the year to date with percentages as in Table 3.3, and second, by giving the variance and percentage variance between the actuals and both the budget and last year's figure for the month and year to date as in Table 3.4.

Table 3.3 The headings on monthly management accounting reports in case study B

This month			Cumulative		
Actual %	Budget %	Last Yr %	Actual %	Budget %	Last Yr %
£'000	£'000	£'000	£'000	£'000	£'000

Table 3.4 The headings on monthly management accounting reports in case study C

Month of April			12 months to date		
	Variance			Variance	
Actual	Budget	Last Yr	Actual	Budget	Last Yr
£'000	£'000 %	£'000 %	£'000 %	£'000 %	£'000 %

An exception to the lack of use of standard costs was found in B. The management had taken active steps to study cost behaviour in order to identify the standard costs for food, beverages and the labour input required to service operations for different levels of activity. The resultant standards are intended to assist cost control, particularly labour costs. It is intended in due course to extend the control exercise to indirect labour costs. In essence, subject to a minimum core workforce which is a fixed cost, the concept is to view and get management to accept that labour costs are actively manageable variable costs which can be changed as occupancy and other activity levels change. The cost standards are set at standard business unit level. This use of management accounting for decision-making was seen as a strong cultural change from historical report-based management accounting practice to a pro-active role.

At board level, the information was typically profits summarised at brand level with additional backing detail for individual hotels in large groups or merely the profits of each hotel in smaller groups, comparison of the actuals on a period and cumulative basis being compared with the same items for last year and from the budget. Head office costs and financial charges are deducted from the profits to arrive at the group trading profit before tax. Table 3.5 shows an example of the weekly group net profit summary adapted from D.

Table 3.5 Management accounting information for the board

GROUP NET PROFIT SUMMARY
Individual hotels' or the results of branded groups of hotels' trading profit

TOTAL TRADING PROFIT
HEAD OFFICE COSTS
  Administrative and General
  Sales and marketing
  Personnel
  Audit
  Other
TOTAL ADMINISTRATION CHARGES
Financial charges
GROUP NET TRADING PROFIT

As well as financial data the management accounting systems in all the case studies also produced non-financial data. For example, at C the following key statistics were reported: room occupancy percentage, average daily room rate, and yield per available room (the latter is the product of the others). At B, the non-financial statistics included not only room occupancy and average room rate but also percentage margins on food, beverages and telephone.

3.2 *Central cost allocation*

The extent to which head office costs (covering areas as diverse as central reservation services, brochures, training, advice, marketing, and personnel) were charged to individual hotels also varied. There was general agreement with the position put forward by A to the effect that a charge is made for costs directly attributable to a hotel, such as television licences, stocktaking fees, and credit card fees. This is consistent with the textbook position of charging divisions for a variety of central services where the consumption can be controlled even if the price cannot (e.g. *Emmanuel et al.* (1990)) but not charging for general central overheads. For these items the division can control neither consumption nor price and an 'incorrigible'[1] allocation method must be used. However, the degree of charging for central services consumed was not subject to precise boundaries. Thus, at E, there was no charge for head office services, and at D there was no charge for head office services except for brochures. At C consideration was being given to departing from the general rule of not charging for head office services by introducing a charge for services which are ancillary to the main support functions and where alternative local sources are available (e.g. consultancy advice). The hierarchical structure of B led to a greater charging for services both at hotel level and within standard business units. Thus, the costs of the administrative support groups were charged to hotels but hotels were not generally charged for head office services, although such costs may be allocated at the brands level. This approach was justified on the grounds that support function costs are largely fixed and that charging might lead to behaviour that is sub-optimal in group terms, a point well illustrated at A where a policy of charging for training costs was abandoned because charging was found to discourage hotels from sending staff on training courses.

However, there were examples of central costs being allocated through a levy, with sales being the usual 'incorrigible' base. In C, there was a levy to cover the costs of the group marketing department and its activities which was paid for by a single rate, fixed-percentage levy on the budgeted turnover of each of the hotels. At F, the head office imposed a levy based upon budgeted sales to cover both training and marketing costs. The case study with the most comprehensive allocation of costs was B, where standard levies on the budgeted turnover of hotels were imposed for sales and marketing, and personnel management including training and maintenance. The reasons given for the standard levies was that they were imposed to ensure that adequate funds were devoted to key areas and that a centralised approach would improve the value obtained from the expenditure. These reasons are in contrast to the observations of *Zimmerman* (1979), who suggested that the levies might serve either as a means of constraining a manager's consumption of perquisites or be necessary due to 'the difficult to observe' nature of the costs.

In general, the approach in allocating head office overheads conforms with theory with the exception of levies for marketing and training. In the former case, it is viewed as a charge for services rendered in terms of promotion and central bookings which cannot sensibly be linked with individual hotels on a usage or benefits

---

1 The term 'incorrigible' was used by Thomas (1974) to indicate that any method of allocation of such costs is unverifiable and irrefutable.

basis. In the latter instance, charging based on usage may result in a lack of take up of courses, which may in turn impact on uniform standards of service and be detrimental to the brand image and the customer's perception of the group generally.

3.3 *Pricing*

Pricing in the hotel industry is a complex area, as there will be separate prices for a range of interlinked and interdependent services which have very different characteristics. Prices will be required for: accommodation, both bedrooms and conference rooms; ancillary room services like telephone and video films; restaurant food and room service food; beverages; leisure facilities; and other items. Such price discrimination involves two main pricing strategies: (i) segmented markets; and (ii) service bundling.[2] In the case studies, the following segmented lines of business, each with different prices or range of prices, were typically present: rack rates[3] for private customers, although even for this customer group there might be the opportunity of discounts; corporate business split between national (agreements negotiated by head office) and local (agreements negotiated by the hotel locally); and conference rates. Services were also bundled, as for example in the case of the free use of leisure facilities for all guests or in full- or half-board terms and bargain breaks. As *Dorward* (1987) comments, the pricing strategies which would be pursued in environments where markets are segmented and the products may be bundled would centre on the development of distinct market segments and bundles where price skimming can be exercised in order to maximise revenue. This may explain moves towards the branding activities of various hotel groups. Interestingly, the hotel industry was the focus of the only empirical analysis of the effect of buyer preferences when facing bundled goods. *Goldberg et al.* (1984) obtained guests' valuations of hotel amenities (e.g. pool, games room, video service, etc.) and averaged all guests' valuations for a predictor of their preferences for various bundles of amenities. The results found that the guests' valuations of individual services were poor predictors of preferences for specified bundles of amenities. Therefore the presumption that buyers evaluate bundles by summing the value of

---

2 For a discussion of pricing in segmented markets and product bundling, see Dorward (1987).

3 The published tariff (the term being derived from the price displayed in the rack).

the individual amenity prices is not supported. The probable reason for this is that many of the amenities are substitutes or complements for each other.

In all the case studies, pricing policy was essentially market driven along the lines suggested by pricing theory. Thus, pricing was a central part of marketing strategy, with management accounting currently making little contribution. In general, no cost information was provided by management accounting for either rack rates in individual hotels or promotion prices. These findings are consistent with those of *Fitzgerald et al.* (1990) who observed that 'only professional services appear to use costs routinely for pricing decisions'. However, in A, consideration was being given to costing promotion prices through a comparison of revenue and direct costs for stays of various durations.

The main source of variation between the case studies was in the degree of central control exercised over the pricing policy of individual hotels. Typically, promotion and bargain break prices were determined centrally following limited discussions with hotel general managers. General managers had a greater input into the determination of rack rates. The rates were also set following close consultation with the general manager so that his expertise in local market conditions could be input to the decision. The degree and source of input from the centre varied. In A, B, D, E and F, the rates were set with strong input from the centre, but in C pricing policy was left to the discretion of the general managers of each hotel subject to close review when budgets were set. The parties to the decision generally included the managing director, marketing, and finance, but in certain cases the parties involved were more limited. For example, in A the rates were set primarily in conjunction with the marketing department, while in D rates were set following discussions with the managing director and internal advisers.

The involvement of the centre extended in most instances to discounting policy. For example, F issued strict guidelines on discounting from rack rates, and only in C and E were the actual prices charged left to the discretion of individual managers.

All the case study interviewees stressed that the objective of pricing policy was to maximise revenue as direct costs are low (especially for letting rooms) and fixed costs high. The decisions are complicated by factors like the segmentation of the market and the bundling of services, and the existence of real opportunity costs if the hotel is full with discounted customers and full rack rate customers are turned away. All the accountancy functions concentrated on balancing the occupancy percentage with the average room rate in order to maximise revenue, while also bearing in mind the knock-on effect of occupancy rate on additional income from telephone, food, beverage and other sources, and on staffing costs.

In response to the conundrum, E was installing a computerised yield management system, which had been derived from examples in the airline industry. The expert system worked by referencing past experience and required a minimum of twelve months' data. On a continuous basis, the system scans historic experience and advises management on the rate to quote on the basis that rates must fall the nearer the current date gets to the actual date. For example, the system may advise that a booking two months out should get no discount to rack rate, while a booking one day before should receive a discount of 30 per cent. The approach is a price-skimming strategy where one price is charged in each time period but between price periods the price is progressively reduced as the price discriminator moves sequentially through segments of progressively increasing demand elasticity. The system assumes that the past is a reliable guide to the future, with the advice being given in the light of historic experience.

The use of cost information in pricing was confined to the food and beverages areas. In B and D, the role of cost information was to enable the gross margin targets to be met at the price levels dictated by the market. For example, cost information on menu items was used to compile menus which yielded the required gross margin at the set price. In general, these exercises used marginal rather than full costs, with labour being treated as a fixed cost. However, it was only in F that consideration was being given to greater sophistication in the area of pricing food, with the objective of maximising yield rather than merely achieving an agreed margin. Progress in this exercise was hampered by a lack of information on the demand function of the hotel's customers.

The other frequently quoted role of management accounting information in pricing was in sensitivity analysis to ascertain the effect on performance of different pricing structures.

The findings on pricing decisions are at variance with the survey results obtained by *Mills and Sweeting* (1988). These researchers reported that full/ absorption costing was widely used in both manufacturing and service companies in normal circumstances, and that market conditions were only an additional factor in determining prices. Further, by using marginal costs in decision-making, the hotel accounting practitioners avoid the criticisms of commentators like *Bloom et al.* (1984) to the effect that practitioners have a functional fixation with absorption costing.

3.4 Summary

The costing systems were found to be based on marginal costs, but often little effort was put into identifying all marginal costs since margins were extremely high and there was an overriding objective to maximise sales. The other characteristics were a departmental approach to the measurement of performance, a separation of costs into controllable and uncontrollable costs, and a focus on wage costs. In the latter case, although only one case had developed labour standards, all cases stressed the tight control of wage costs and their relationship to activity levels as a primary concern.

Pricing was a complex area given the bundled nature of the services provided and the distinct market segments in a hotel. Prices were found to be driven almost entirely by market forces, as might be anticipated given that there is open information about prices (as discussed in Chapter 2).

4

Management Accounting for Control

4.1 Introduction

A major part of the day-to-day operations of the management accounting function in the hotel groups examined was budgetary planning and control. *Emmanuel et al.* (1990) suggested that the possible role of a budget included: a system of authorisation; a means of forecasting and planning; a channel of communication and co-ordination; a motivational device; a means of performance evaluation and control; and a basis for decision-making. Elements of all these roles were universally present in the budgets of these organisations. However, in some groups where a large proportion of the business was generated locally co-ordination was often not of major importance because of the stand-alone nature of individual hotels.

The budgeting process typically involved two interlinked activities: the long-term budget which covered from three to five years forward, and the annual budget covering twelve months or thirteen four-week periods.

4.2 Long-term budgets

The long-term budgets were updated annually on a rolling basis within the annual budget cycle, so that the first year of the long-term budget equated with the annual budget for the following year.[1] In A, B and C, the planning exercise looked five years forward, whereas in E and F the process was limited to three years forward. The long-term budgets typically covered the balance sheet, profit and loss account, and cash flow statement, and was

---

1   The exception to this was D, which did not formally prepare long-term budgets.

built up on a hotel-by-hotel basis. There was general agreement that certainly beyond two years forward the figures were very speculative, but it was still felt that the exercise was a worthwhile aid to forecasting and planning.

The preparation of the long-term budget usually involved forecasts at hotel level of key elements. These included occupancy percentage and average room rate and the link between these, and the gross margin obtained from other activities. Table 4.1 indicates the level of detail given in the long-term budget of a hotel in A.

The exercise covered five years split into quarters. Assumptions were made in the following four areas to arrive at the profit and loss account:

(i) *Revenue:* occupancy percentage; average room rate; rooms revenue as a percentage of total revenue; food revenue as a percentage of total revenue; beverage revenue as a percentage of total revenue; room hire as a percentage of total revenue; and supplementary revenue as a percentage of total revenue.

(ii) *Margin:* rooms gross margin; food gross margin; beverage gross margin; room hire gross margin; and supplementary gross margin.

(iii) *Expenses:* salaries and wages as a percentage of total revenue; establishment costs as a percentage of total revenue; sales and marketing costs as a percentage of total revenue; overheads as a percentage of total revenue; and hotel depreciation as a percentage of total revenue.

(iv) *Sundries:* cash/BC/Access sales as a percentage of total revenue; Amex/Diners sales as a percentage of total revenue; and credit account sales as a percentage of total revenue.

The balance sheet required assumptions in the following 3 areas:

(i) *Current capital:* purchase price for hotel; NBV or valuation of hotel; number of bedrooms at acquisition; acquisition costs as a percentage of purchase price; extensions (total building cost and number of bedrooms built); other capital expenditure; and total sale proceeds of entire disposal.

(ii) *Opening working capital:* book value of stock; book value of debtors (Amex/Diners); book value of debtors (credit accounts); book value of creditors; closing stock levels; annual rate of increase in stock levels (%); receipt period for debtors (days); Amex/Diners sales;

Table 4.1 Long-term budget for an individual hotel

X Hotel: long-term budget

Hotel profit and loss account

Yr 1 Q1   *Yr 1 Q2*   *etc...*

Room revenue
Food revenue
Beverage revenue
Room hire revenue
Supplementary revenue

TOTAL HOTEL TURNOVER

Operating expenses:
  rooms
  food
  beverage
  room hire
  supplementary
Total operating expenses

GROSS MARGIN

Gross margin – % to total hotel turnover

Salaries and wages
Establishment costs
Sales and marketing costs
Overheads
Depreciation
Total indirect expenses

NET HOTEL PROFIT

Net hotel profit – % to total hotel turnover

Cash sales
Credit card sales
Company account sales
Analysis of total hotel turnover
Salaries and wages – % to total hotel turnover

credit accounts; payment period for creditors (days); food and beverage.
(iii) *Capital expenditure assumptions:* cumulative number of rooms purchased; cumulative number of room extensions; number of rooms disposed of; number of rooms available to generate income; number of rooms capitalised; acquisition cost per room; finished extension cost per room; and acquisition expenses.

As discussed in Chapter 2, the long-term budgets were essentially a strategic device which allowed management to explore the impact of a range of strategies under a number of different scenarios on the balance sheet, profit and loss account and cash flows. Particular emphasis was placed on identifying future funding requirements, and planning how the group through acquisitions, disposals and other activities could alter its shape to meet various corporate long-term objectives and the impact of these on financial performance and structure.

4.3 The annual budget cycle

The length of the budget cycle varied from around six months down to three months. A, B and C had the longest cycles. For A, the long cycle arose because budget preparation was combined with a forecast of the outcome for the current year. In the case of B, the five-month cycle probably reflected the complex structure of the organisation and the international component of the business, while for C the long cycle allows for a prolonged negotiation prior to the budget being finalised and, again, the international nature of the group. The shorter cycles in E and F reflect the comparatively smaller number of hotels in these groups and the pressures of timetables imposed by the parent company; while the shorter cycle in D reflects the bottom-up approach to the budgeting process.

4.4 The annual budget process

This chapter follows the preparation of the group budget from the viewpoint of head office rather than discussing budget preparation within the hotel. Thus, the responsibility centre is the hotel and not the cost or profit centres within the hotel. Budget preparation broadly followed the textbook practices (see, for example, *Edey* (1966) or *Arnold and Hope* (1990)). Among the six case studies there were examples of top-down, interative and bottom-up approaches to preparing budgets. The majority of cases followed an iterative process. The extent of consultation and the procedures for negotiation varied. In C, E and F the interative process was fairly involved, while in A the negotiations were limited.

In C, the iterative process involved considerable interaction between head office management and the hotel. The process commences with a bottom-up input from the hotels as each hotel is asked to provide for review by head office details of its forecast occupancy percentages by class of business, average room rates by class of business, and a sales and marketing plan. The figures are used to produce an initial budget for each hotel. Overseas hotels budget in their local currency and this is converted at a standard rate by head office.

Once the initial budget is prepared each hotel is visited by a head office member of the finance staff who reviews the budget with the hotel management line by line for one to two days. The finance director described this process as 'a professional game' in which the reviewer needed to be aware of linkages between revenue and expenditure. The areas of disagreement which cannot be resolved at this stage are identified and highlighted for discussion at the next stage. This stage involves a meeting between the the hotel general manager together with any staff he may wish to bring along and a committee from head office comprising the chief executive, the head of sales and marketing and the finance director. The finance director observed that the most common difficulty was persuading hotel general managers to raise prices in response to cost increases. The committee reviews the budget and the report of the reviewing accountant from head office. By the end of the meeting disputed areas should have been resolved so that the hotel can produce a final budget. This operation covers about three hotels a day.

The budgets were prepared at a very detailed level over the main departments (rooms, food and beverage, communications, and other expenses) and the major overhead areas (administration and general, advertising and promotion, energy, and repairs and maintenance). Costs were analysed into fixed and variable. For example, the rooms department budget was built up for each line of business (rack rate, corporate–national (agreements negotiated by head office), corporate–local (agreements negotiated locally), conference, etc.) with relevant expenses analysed into those that varied with room occupancy levels (laundry, cleaning, linen, etc.) which were costs per room sold, and those that were fixed (TV licences, equipment rental, etc.). A similar level of detail was employed for below-the-line items like administration and general. The final budgets were consolidated and the head office budget was added to give a budget for the group which is finalised after agreement with the parent. The final budget covers the balance sheet, profit and loss account and cash flow.

At F, the corporate plan developed earlier and discussion with the group centre is a starting-point. The group head office also provides forecasts of key economic indicators like inflation and changes in consumer spending. These statistics were communicated to the general managers preparing the budget of individual hotels, though they were rarely of much use as local conditions vary. Beyond these inputs, the initial budgets were prepared without any direct input from head office in order to involve the managers in the process and because local managers were considered the best judges of the local situation and market pressures. The individual hotels sent in budgets which included all cost and revenue lines. After a preliminary screening by the finance director, the hotels were consolidated and the budget for the head office functions and the interest rate for borrowing, as dictated by group head office, added in order to give a position for the division. Vital to determining the head office budget was the capital and maintenance audit to estimate improvements, repairs, and renewals necessary to maintain standards in hotels. The outcome was compared with the corporate planning exercise. The managing director and finance director carried out a detailed scrutiny of each hotel's budget with the hotel manager. As a result of this two or three revisions take place before a final budget is arrived at.

At E, the iterative process was more top down as the new budget cycle began with a briefing meeting between head office and the general managers at which the procedures were discussed, and guidelines and pro forma budgets issued. The guidelines are based on information issued by the parent, which covered a review of economic, demographic and market trends relevant in the hotel industry. Of particular relevance are: (i) forecasts of long-term interest rates, consumer spending, labour market trends, leisure spending trends and sector demand trends; and (ii) hotel sector-specific data on a national and regional basis covering average room rates, room stock, occupancy rates and hotel operating ratios. The hotel general managers were required to complete the pro forma on a Lotus disk which was in the format of Table 4.2 overleaf.

A prime source of revenue data was the booking system, which provided a historic record of revenue by origin code (type of revenue). The initial profit target was submitted by the hotel as it was felt it was important that the hotel general manager should be committed to this initial target. Experience suggested that general managers set quite ambitious targets through an eagerness to please. From this point the group management accountant described the reviewer's role as 'judging but disassociated'. The hotel budgets were consolidated with the head office function budgets to provide an initial company position. The budgets were reviewed by the accounting function and operations staff and submitted to head office, who refined the budget further before the budget targets were finalised. The budget summary was prepared by completing detailed sheets for each department and each main overhead grouping. Costs of sales are deducted from the total to give the gross profit split by department. From the gross profit is deducted departmental employment costs and other departmental costs to arrive at the total departmental contribution, against which is offset central and other allocated overheads to arrive at profit before and after rent.

Outside this formal budgeting system, hotels were encouraged to undertake weekly and monthly forecasts. The forecasts, which involved staff from the main hotel departments, covered the current month in weekly detail, the next month in less detail and two further months at an overviewed level. The forecast system and the involvement of hotel staff relates to an 'Investors in People Initiative'. The predictions are compared with actuals on a weekly basis, the variances investigated and understood and the budgets are rolled forward on a monthly basis. The forecasts of the hotel general managers are consolidated on a monthly basis.

A similar procedure was followed at A, where hotels were asked to complete Lotus 1-2-3 standard pro forma worksheets on a disk. With the disks are instructions on how they should be completed and 'economic' information provided by the marketing department to assist with the assessment of economic activity in the hotel market in the next year. The hotel used the worksheet to provide a forecast to the year-end and for the following year, which had to be returned completed by the individual hotels. After examination at

Table 4.2 The format of the operating statement in case study E

	Month 1	Month 2	etc

SALES
Accommodation
Other rooms and telephone
Restaurants/food
Bars
Leisure club
Golf

Total sales

COST OF SALES
Rooms and telephone
Restaurants/food
Bars
Leisure club
Golf

Total gross profit

DEPARTMENTAL EMPLOYMENT COSTS
Rooms and telephone
Restaurants/food
Bars
Leisure club
Golf
Administrative and general

DEPARTMENTAL EXPENSES
Rooms and telephone
Restaurants/food
Bars
Leisure club
Golf

Total departmental contributions

GENERAL OVERHEADS
Laundry
Legal costs and licences
Printing, stationery and computers
Sundries
Promotional and advertising
Repairs and renewals
Utilities
Depreciation

Total general overheads

HOTEL PROFIT

head office and visits by the management accountant to hotels, the hotels disks are returned to hotels to enable them to update their forecasts with actuals and make agreed revisions to the budget. The revised budgets were consolidated with the head office support function budget. The resultant consolidated forecast position in terms of balance sheet, profit and loss account and cash flow statement for the company and budget were submitted to the board for approval.

The approach at B was largely top down as opposed to bottom up because in most hotels the business generated centrally by the company is dominant. The annual budget cycle was based on the consolidation of the budgets of the standard business units (SBUs). The process commenced with the issuing of budget frameworks to the SBUs which contained details of the budgeted revenues from centrally controlled sources such as leisure breaks, overseas trade and centrally negotiated commercial agreements. The SBUs in conjunction with the individual hotels expanded the framework by including local information based on their expectations of the local business market, casual trade, other restaurant, and the health and fitness centre markets. The variable cost parts of the budget were estimated by the SBUs and negotiated at a hotel level and checked against the cost standards. Fixed costs were based on best estimates on a hotel-by-hotel basis. A similar approach was adopted for overseas hotels except that all the amounts were in local currency with all currency conversion effects being accounted for at the brand level.

At D, the approach was largely bottom up. The draft budgets were completed at hotels and sent to head office for scrutiny. Each hotel general manager had a meeting with the managing director, operations director and chief accountant at which the budget was discussed in detail. The discussion set in process a revision of the budget through the interaction of operations and sales and marketing to reduce excess capacity and produce a revised budget at hotel level. For example, periods of low occupancy would be identified and attempts made to fill the rooms with tour parties which were organised centrally. The revised budgets of the hotels were consolidated together with budgets for the head office functions to provide the group budget for the year split into thirteen periods of four weeks.

4.5 *The aim of the budget*

The budget may be set as a target that management are motivated to meet, a realistic forecast of the likely outcome, or some combination of these goals. For budgets to be effective motivational targets, *Hofstede* (1968) and others have suggested that the targets must be accepted by the budget holder, and this would usually be achieved with a bottom-up or iterative approach. Among the case studies, only D set budgets principally as a forecast. This approach reflects the 'paternalistic' style of senior management and the close supervision of hotel general managers by senior management. In A and B, the approach was very different. In the former, the budget was a clear target which general managers and head office management were expected to meet. In the latter, the company allowed and expected SBUs and the hotels under them to fix budgets that it deemed unrealistic. The head office overcame any overstatement in the consolidated position by holding provisions for anticipated shortfalls at the centre. Thus budgets at SBU and hotel level were targets for the managers, while at a consolidated level they were a forecast and target. In contrast, at C, E, and F the budgets were intended to reflect a realistic performance target which it was expected that hotels could meet and the budget is thus both a target and a forecast of the expected outcome. At these companies, this dual approach is in part explained by the need for the companies to provide accurate reports to their parent company head office to maintain the credibility of the senior management. Indeed, so keen was C on providing accurate budgets and forecasts that 'awards' were made to the hotel general managers who were closest to and furthest from the budget and forecast out-turn (management placed greater emphasis on the accuracy of the forecast out-turn than the budget).

4.6 *Variance analysis*

In general, variances were calculated only on a line-by-line basis, with the addition of percentages in some cases. The one exception to this was C, where the information on the percentage variance from the plan for the current week and cumulatively for each period was supplemented, where significant problems were noted, by an analysis of variances into their constituent parts. For example, the rooms variance might be broken down into empty rooms, room occupancy, room sales and average room rates variances across a variety of headings including rack rates, business commercial, conference, group travel and leisure breaks; the food variance might be analysed into covers and average spends for different meals.

In all cases, once the budgets had been finalised they remained fixed through the year and thus all variances were against the forecast rather than actual activity. The lack of budget flexing reflects the low marginal cost in all lines of business, the high fixed cost structure of the hotel industry, and a view that revenue was the priority. However, in E, there was a forecasting system which co-existed with the formal budgeting system, where hotels were encouraged to undertake weekly and monthly forecasts (see p.43).

4.7 Summary

In all the cases considerable time and effort were expended by accounting staff and hotel and head office management in drawing up and agreeing annual budgets. The budgets fulfilled several roles, which included authorisation for the hotel general manager to incur various overhead costs; forecasting and planning both in the short and longer term; acting as a channel of communication and co-ordination, especially in hotels which were reliant on the head office for a high proportion of business; motivating staff in at least some of the hotels; a means of performance evaluation and control (as discussed in Chapter 5) ; and a basis for decision-making, especially in investment appraisal exercises (as discussed in Chapter 6).

Table 4.3 overleaf summarises the approach for each of the case companies. Long-term budgets extending from three to five years and prepared at a high level were the norm. The budget cycle varies depending on the approach and the number of hotels in the group.

The budgets were typically fixed iteratively. Head office would supply the individual hotels with economic and marketing data and a standard pro forma for completion. The various meetings between the hotel general manager and senior management would take place before a final version was agreed. The process made full use of information technology, with budget frameworks being issued as standard spreadsheet packages on a diskette or electronically. The analysis of variances was done on a line-by-line basis and in general budgets were not flexed.

Most variations in approach arose from the degree of interaction between head office and the hotel and the extent to which the budget was a target as opposed to a forecast.

Table 4.3 Summary of management accounting for control

Company	Long-term budgets	Time horizon (years)	Length of budget cycle	Preparation of the budget
A	Yes	5	long	Iterative
B	Yes	5	long	Top-down
C	Yes	5	long	Iterative
D	No	n/a	short	Bottom-up
E	Yes	3	short	Iterative
F	Yes	3	short	Iterative

5

Performance Evaluation in the Hotel Industry

5.1 Introduction

Emmanuel, Otley and Merchant (1990) argue that there is an important distinction to be made between decision situations which are sufficiently well understood for reliable predictions of the decision outcome to be made, and those where one has to rely on the judgement of managers because there is no formal mechanism for predicting decision outcomes. The former category are termed *programmed decisions* while the latter are called *non-programmed decisions*. This dichotomy is, like many such binary categorisations, a simplifying abstraction; more realistically, as Emmanuel et al. note, the model can be thought of as a continuum. This concept of programmed and non-programmed decisions is useful in the hotel industry as most decisions taken tend towards the programmed rather than non-programmed end of the continuum.

The investment decision is described in more detail in Chapter 6. However, we note here that the principal investment decisions are new builds, extensions of hotels (both in terms of expansion and new facilities), acquisition of existing hotels, and divestments. In general, the decisions on all except extensions are made at hotel head office level (although usually subject to board approval), while extension projects can be initiated at head office or hotel level. In virtually all cases, the type of business operation is well understood, with predictable cost behaviour patterns; demand is, of course, more difficult to forecast but causality factors are well defined and researchable.[1] Thus, investment decisions are certainly more 'programmed' than, say, those found in manufacturing industry with the launch of a completely new product. This is largely because the hotel industry, like other service businesses such as

---

1 See Chapter 6.

retail outlets, allows what we might term 'expansion through experience'. Management effectively learns through the collective experience of existing projects and can therefore make reasonable predictions about new hotel projects.

At the operating level, the principal decisions concern short-run tactical pricing and marketing (e.g. what discounts need to be offered to obtain optimal occupancy), and the matching of staffing levels to occupancy. The fact that these decisions are essentially 'programmed' is attested to by the fact that one of our companies, E, was experimenting with an expert system based upon an airline booking system.[2]

Given that, at hotel level, decisions tend to be at the 'programmed' end of the spectrum, it may be expected that budgetary controls feature strongly in the performance evaluation of hotel managers, and this turns out to be the case. The theory of responsibility accounting would also suggest that the more autonomy a manager has, the more he or she may be appraised on the basis of hotel profits or even hotel return on capital employed. Both of these measures are used in the appraisal process, although the latter measure is only used by one of our companies (E).

An important issue in many service industries is performance in non-financial terms. *Fitzgerald et al.* (1991) view hotels as 'service shop' businesses. They claim that such businesses need performance measures across five dimensions besides that of financial performance. These are: competitiveness; quality of service; flexibility; resource utilisation; and innovation. In general, we found that our sample companies tended to be active in measuring competitiveness, quality of service and resource utilisation. In the hotel industry, resource utilisation and 'volume flexibility' (defined by Fitzgerald et al. to be the ability to respond to changes in demand) tend to be facets of the same thing, given that the basic room resource is fixed and that the short-run objective is centred upon the maximisation of room revenue. The other flexibility measures proposed by Fitzgerald et al. are 'specification flexibility', the degree to which the service process can be adapted to meet individual customer needs, and 'delivery speed flexibility', which in a hotel would only apply to peripheral services such as check-in queueing, room service waiting time, and

---

2 See 'Pricing' in Chapter 3.

so on. These tended to be considered as aspects of service quality. Innovation was not measured as such, although the financial and non-financial results of innovations such as the addition of leisure facilities were measured.

A further issue in performance evaluation is the linkage between 'rewards' and performance. 'Rewards' is a very general term, and can be defined to cover cash or cash-equivalent sums (bonuses), prospect improvements (such as promotions or increased likelihood of future salary rises), non-financial rewards, and 'negative rewards' such as dismissal and demotion. All of these appeared in our survey, with some companies being heavily 'incentivised' (notably, firms who thus described themselves invariably meant cash bonuses), while others were quite hostile towards the idea of bonuses. This hostility was typically based upon past experience of bonus systems and a view that they encouraged 'short-termism'.

When discussing 'performance evaluation', it was clear that in general the concern was with the evaluation of the general manager and his results against what could reasonably be expected, rather than of the business unit. However, the head office function also reviewed the profitability of individual hotels, and inadequate performance could give rise to the consideration of closure and/or disposal of the unit. The analysis used in disposal decisions is discussed in Chapter 6.

We now examine each of these areas (measurement of financial performance, measurement of non-financial performance, and rewards) in turn.

5.2 *Measurement of financial performance*

Individual hotels can broadly be viewed as stand-alone divisions. In principle, all our sample companies took this approach in so far as some aspect of profit performance was measured at hotel level. Some of our sample companies went further and measured profit at departmental level, although the use of cost allocations in this process varied between companies.[3] The literature on the appraisal of the financial performance of divisions is extensive, with there being some agreement that if the divisional manager has either

---

3 See Chapter 3.

control or influence over the investment base of his or her division, the inclusion of some number reflecting the opportunity cost of capital employed is desirable.[4] Although, in practice, return on investment (ROI) seems to be the preferred measure (*Reece and Cool* (1978), *Tomkins* (1973)), the academic literature exhibits concern with the problems of ROI. *Tomkins* (1973) points out that a residual income measure is preferable, provided depreciation is properly specified. In the case of projects with constant cash flows, 'properly specified' can be taken as meaning the use of annuity depreciation.[5] Unfortunately, with non-constant cash flows Tomkins argues that economic depreciation, incorporating the present values of future cash flows of the individual assets, must be used. As he points out, this is inconvenient because, *inter alia*, such depreciation and asset valuation is in contravention of generally accepted accounting principles. Tomkins shows that one way around this problem, which is particularly relevant for our purposes, is to appraise divisional manager performance on the basis of the difference between planned cash flows at the time of project proposal, and ex post cash flows.[6] In all companies where there was some formal investment appraisal process involving the estimation of future cash flows or profits (all companies except D), the planned cash flows proposed by hotel managers wishing to expand their hotels were incorporated into the following year's cash flows, and into longer-run strategic budgets where used. As Tomkins shows, this is equivalent to measuring residual income on the increase in the asset base resulting from the new investment.

On new builds and new acquisitions a similar process was followed, the only difference being that the planned cash flows originated wholly from head office, as opposed to some joint process involving hotel and head office management.[7] Thus, on new investment, financial performance (at least in the first year following the inception of the project) is measured in a way compatible with that suggested in the literature.

---

4   For a summary of these arguments, see Gregory (1988).

5   For cash flows constant in real terms, an inflation-adjusted version of annuity depreciation can be used.

6   Gregory (1987), noting some limitations of this method, proposes the alternative of head office leasing assets to divisions, with the lease charge calculated so as to spread the NPV of the project through time pro rata to its planned cash flows. Such an approach could readily be applied to the hotel industry, especially if activities were divided between property and management as described in Chapter 6.

7   Except in the case of B; see Chapter 6.

Turning to the more general issue of financial performance measurement, only company E made any attempt to measure ROI. More typically, performance measurement concentrated on budgeted versus actual profit. There are key differences between companies in the way that budgeted profit is arrived at. In some firms it is clearly specified as a target rather than as an expectation, while there are differences in the participation of managers in the budget-setting process, and further differences in the degree of emphasis placed upon meeting the budget.

In A, a target profit negotiated between head office and the individual hotel managers in the planning process is the key performance measure. Return on capital employed measures are not used explicitly, but profit expectations reflect the resources employed and depreciation is charged in arriving at the profit target.

The management accounting section produces a weekly performance league table with an emphasis on revenue for each of the hotels. The position in the table is based on percentage variance from the plan, and data is provided both for the current week and cumulatively for each period. The report covers rooms, room hire, beverages, food, leisure, and sundry sales. Where significant problems are noted the variances can be analysed into their constituent parts – for example, the room variance can be broken down into empty rooms, room occupancy, room sales and average room rates variances across a variety of headings including rack rates, business commercial, conference, group travel and leisure breaks; and the food variance can be analysed into covers and average spends for different meals.

In B, the approach is largely top down as opposed to bottom up because in most hotels the business generated centrally by the company is dominant. The company allows and expects strategic business units (SBU) to fix budgets at the top of the range of expectations and holds provisions for anticipated shortfalls at the centre. Thus budgets are targets for both the SBUs and individual hotels. There are no automatic penalties for failing to meet budget but performance against budget is a key element in appraising manager performance.

As the actual figures arise forecasts of the outcome for a period ahead are prepared. The forecasts are prepared for three time periods:

(i) Five weeks ahead – the forecast is based on what business there is on the books and ensures that the rostering of staff is based on this level. If business exceeds this level, there is a formula which allows a limited amount of additional staff to be employed. In essence the approach is pessimistic and aims to control wages costs.

(ii) Four-month rolling forecast – this forecast is aimed at a realistic assessment of the level of trading which is sent up to the group executive.

(iii) Extend the forecast forward to the half year or year end. In practice, this means forecasting up to a maximum of eight months forward.

Performance against (i) and (ii) for the current month is updated weekly and is sales- and wages-driven on the assumption that other costs can be delivered at the budget figure. The forecasts enable performance against the hotel profit contribution and profit before interest and tax to be tracked on a weekly basis.

The main performance measures (besides performance against budget) are the room yield (average rate multiplied by occupancy percentage) and hotel profit contribution, which derives from the gross profit figures for each of the profit centres (rooms; catering; health and fitness centres; and other including phones, banqueting, conferences and retail outlets). The costs deducted in arriving at the hotel profit contribution are controllable costs including direct and indirect labour and also non-controllable costs like rates, insurance and depreciation, but not rent which is mainly related to centrally driven financing decisions. The key performance measures are compared with the budget and previous year figures both for the same month and cumulative year to date. In reviewing performance half the focus is on variance against the current year and half on last year's performance. There is a monthly performance review at individual hotel level both at head office and the SBU.

Cash targets are also set for individual hotels. Cash control focuses on hotel profit contribution plus depreciation less capital spend and plus or minus stock and debtor changes. No other cash movements are attributed to individual units.

In contrast to the top-down approach adopted at B, in C the budget is negotiated in meetings between head office and hotel managers. By the end of these meetings disputed areas should have been resolved so that the hotel can produce a final budget. Interestingly, the finance director described the process by saying 'budgeting is a professional game'.[8] Again by contrast with B, the budgets are intended to reflect a realistic performance target which it is expected that hotels will meet. In part this is explained by the need of the company to provide accurate reports to head office, but it also reflects a less centralised management style in a smaller organisation with direct contact between hotel general managers and head office. The emphasis on accurate forecasting is confirmed in the process of holding quarterly meetings of all the hotel general managers, with awards for the hotel which is closest to budget and booby prizes for the furthest from budget. General managers also receive detailed statistics on their performance covering critical items like occupancy percentages, average room rates and profits for comparison with other hotels in the group.

Performance against the budget is monitored monthly, with detailed information based on a spreadsheet that is provided by each hotel to head office by the sixth working day following the month end. This enables a fully consolidated group position to be obtained by the seventh working day. The actual results are compared both against budget and the previous year's figures on both monthly and cumulative bases but the emphasis is on the comparison against budget. For overseas hotels, performance is measured in local currency terms but information is also provided on the sterling outcome. The returns are considered at a monthly board meeting on the tenth working day. In addition to this budget cycle, weekly cash reports are received and compared with the cash budget. This forms a basis for cash transfers to head office. The budgets and performance appraisal include some qualitative measures like occupancy percentages and sleepers, but in general financial performance is the crucial measure. Performance is not measured against capital employed except at the project appraisal stage.

In D, investment appraisal was characterised by an informal process, but this was not true of performance measurement. Performance evaluation is based on hotel net profit performance, where net profit is gross profit less labour costs, other expenses, and repairs and renewals (which includes depreciation), with

---

8 This should not be taken as implying that budgeting is not taken seriously in C. Rather, it illustrates the awareness of the finance director of the behavioural issues arising in the negotiating of budgetary targets.

comparisons of this actual net profit with budget and last year. Particular emphasis is placed on occupancy rates and labour costs to turnover. The former focuses on revenue maximisation and the latter on the major controllable cost. In this company, the budgeting process was described as being bottom up in construction, with the budgets being forecasts rather than targets.

The monitoring of budget against actuals and previous year results is covered by a four-weekly report for the board which shows: last year (period and cumulative); actual (period and cumulative); and budget (period and cumulative). This is given for each hotel, together with summarised information across different groupings of hotels. Similar information is also produced for the head office functions in order to produce a group net trading profit summary.

For the management of operations, an operating statement for each hotel is produced by the tenth working day after each four-week period, with a detailed split of revenue and costs over room sales, food sales, liquor, tobacco, and sundries. The information focuses not only on net margin but also on a detailed analysis of expenses under operating and repair and renewal headings to arrive at the final net profit. Operating management also focuses on weekly information covering actuals and last year. The head office management will particularly concentrate on sales shortfalls, the relationship between sales activity and wages costs, and the control of operating and other expenses. The review process was described as being 'based upon a teamwork/problem-solving approach'.

In E, besides the use of budgeted versus actual profit as a performance measure, we also found our only evidence of the use of an ROI measure. The performance against budget is measured monthly and corrective action taken on variances. Key performance indicators are net profit after depreciation but before rent payments (where applicable), room occupancy percentage, and achieved room rate. There was participation in budget preparation; budgets are seen as achievable, with managers being encouraged to be 'realistic but positive' in their forecasts. For additional data comparison is made of figures for: YIELD (actual revenue divided by potential revenue which would arise if all rooms were fully let at rack rates); ACCPAR (accommodation per available room); and SALESPAR (total sales per available room). In addition to this monthly monitoring, all hotel general managers meet twice yearly to review company performance together with regional and individual sales and profit targets. At this meeting the pricing and occupancy strategy is closely reviewed.

Another, perhaps more crucial, report for tracking performance is the weekly analysis of hotel performance which covers budget and actual data on sales split by accommodation, food, beverage, and other income; total gross profit based on standard percentages applied to food and beverages; salaries and wages plus wages/income percentage; overheads; and profit. The profit is compared with the budget and the variance calculated. Other statistics are: beds let this year and last year; rooms let this year and last year; room occupancy; and average room rate this year and last year.

In addition to the above, a performance evaluation exercise of individual investments is undertaken annually. Copies are sent to the parent company and each individual hotel general manager. The exercise, which also acts as a review of the efficiency of the capital expenditure for each hotel, covers ten years. The exercise commences with the acquisition value of the hotel and adds in all major projects, refurbishments and other capital expenditure (including capitalised interest costs) to give a total capital expenditure on the hotel. The total capital expenditure is adjusted for annual valuation changes at the annual revaluation and depreciation to arrive at the general ledger book value for each year. This figure is adjusted for changes in the RPI to obtain a real value of the capital expenditure as revalued and depreciated. This figure is used to calculate an ROI based (i) on the profit contribution of hotels (profit before costs not attributed to departments) and (ii) cash flows. Interestingly, as increases in asset values pass through the 'profit' as defined for this evaluation purpose, this is close to the income measure proposed in *Edwards, Kay and Meyer* (1987). It is not, however, exactly equivalent as 'value to the owner' (or deprival value) is not actively considered in the appraisal.

In F, the key performance indicator is budgeted net profit which is after controllable *and* non-controllable expenses. The emphasis on budgeted profit is also revealed in the profit-planning exercises that occur towards the end of the financial year. Usually, six months' actual plus six months' forecast and eight months' actual plus four months' forecast positions are determined as a prelude to preparing a nine months' actual plus three months' forecast for the group head office.

On a shorter timescale, hotels provide weekly performance reports which contain the full profit and loss account with information on the week's results, actual performance in the year to date, and a forecast for the following week. The forecasts are consolidated to obtain the position for the division as a whole. These reports are the key to monitoring the progress of the hotels and initiating corrective action as appropriate.

5.3 *Measurement of non-financial performance*

Given the importance of revenue maximisation in an industry where many of the costs (at least those associated with the room-letting side of the business) are fixed, it is not surprising that some of the key non-financial indicators are associated with occupancy and capacity utilisation. All our sample companies produced statistics in this area. Room occupancy percentages and statistics reflecting average room revenue were common. Further statistical analysis included number of 'sleepers' (as opposed to rooms let) and average additional spending per guest. This type of information is also collected nationally by some of the major consultancies (see Table 2.1). All these statistics can be viewed as measures of resource utilisation or 'volume flexibility' (*Fitzgerald et al.* 1991).

All the companies in our sample were well aware of the importance of quality and the majority, to greater or lesser extents, attempted to measure it. However, the measures used differ between companies; many use guest questionnaires (a typical example is shown in Table 5.1), some utilise 'mystery guests' and in one firm, F, the quality standard forms part of the bonus system (see below).

Turning to the individual companies in detail, the non-financial performance measures used in A included qualitative variables for room occupancy, sleepers and covers, but the context was their impact on revenue. Currently, the management accounting system has no qualitative measures in the areas of quality, flexibility, resource utilisation, and innovation. The proposed revision to the management structure has a director in charge of quality and service. It is anticipated that the management accounting function will be involved in determining suitable measures such as repeat business and an analysis of customer satisfaction questionnaires.

Table 5.1 Sample customer questionnaire

RESERVATION

How did you know about the hotel?

Was the reservation made:
  Directly to the Hotel? ☐
  By (special breaks) Central Reservations? ☐
  By (special breaks) Reservation Office? ☐
  By a travel agent/hotel booking agent? ☐

	Yes	No
Was your reservation handled courteously and quickly?	☐	☐

RECEPTION

	Yes	No
Was your reservation in order on arrival?	☐	☐
If no, was the problem handled to your satisfaction?	☐	☐

How did you rate the:	Excellent	Good	Average	Poor
Courtesy on arrival	☐	☐	☐	☐
Efficiency of check-in	☐	☐	☐	☐
Handling of check-out	☐	☐	☐	☐

QUALITY OF SERVICE

How well did our staff provide you with quality service in these areas?

	Excellent	Good	Average	Poor
Reception	☐	☐	☐	☐
Concierge	☐	☐	☐	☐
Porters	☐	☐	☐	☐
Housekeeping	☐	☐	☐	☐
Room service	☐	☐	☐	☐
Restaurants	☐	☐	☐	☐
Bars	☐	☐	☐	☐
Lounge	☐	☐	☐	☐
Telephone operators	☐	☐	☐	☐
Conference/banqueting	☐	☐	☐	☐
Leisure facilities	☐	☐	☐	☐

Table 5.1 continued

GUEST ROOM

How would you rate the:	Excellent	Good	Average	Poor
Cleanliness	☐	☐	☐	☐
Comfort	☐	☐	☐	☐
Décor	☐	☐	☐	☐
Supplies (towels, soap, hangers etc.) ☐		☐	☐	☐
Facilities	☐	☐	☐	☐

	Yes	No
Was everything in your room in working order?	☐	☐

If no, please state what item and whether the problem was corrected promptly?

RESTAURANT AND BARS

How did you rate:	Excellent	Good	Average	Poor
Service and efficiency?				
Breakfast	☐	☐	☐	☐
Lunch/dinner main restaurant	☐	☐	☐	☐
other restaurant(s) ☐		☐	☐	☐
bars	☐	☐	☐	☐
Quality of food and drink?				
Breakfast	☐	☐	☐	☐
Lunch/dinner main restaurant	☐	☐	☐	☐
other restaurant(s) ☐		☐	☐	☐
bars	☐	☐	☐	☐
Choice of food and drink?				
Breakfast	☐	☐	☐	☐
Lunch/dinner main restaurant	☐	☐	☐	☐
other restaurant(s) ☐		☐	☐	☐
bars	☐	☐	☐	☐

Table 5.1 continued

	Excellent	Good	Average	Poor
Atmosphere?				
Breakfast	☐	☐	☐	☐
Lunch/dinner main restaurant	☐	☐	☐	☐
other restaurant(s)	☐	☐	☐	☐
bars	☐	☐	☐	☐
Value for price paid?				
Breakfast	☐	☐	☐	☐
Lunch/dinner main restaurant	☐	☐	☐	☐
other restaurant(s)	☐	☐	☐	☐
bars	☐	☐	☐	☐

ANY COMMENTS?

Would you like to make any additional comments which could help us to make your next stay more enjoyable?

_____

_____

Which additional facilities/supplies would you like to see available?

_____

_____

GENERAL COMMENTS

	Yes	No
Was this your first visit to:		
an XYZ hotel?	☐	☐
this hotel?	☐	☐
Would you stay again:		
at an XYZ hotel?	☐	☐
at this hotel?	☐	☐

Comments

_____

_____

Table 5.1 *continued*

Overall, would you consider your stay with us:	Yes	No
a pleasant one?	☐	☐
value for money?	☐	☐

Was your stay mainly for:		
business?	☐	☐
conference/meeting/function?	☐	☐
pleasure?	☐	☐

How many overnight business trips have you made during the past year?

0–5	5–10	10–15	15+
☐	☐	☐	☐

	Yes	No
Do you hold an XYZ Corporate Card Scheme?	☐	☐

Your sex:	Male	Female
	☐	☐

Your Age:	16–24	25–34	35–44	45–54	55–64	65+
	☐	☐	☐	☐	☐	☐

Arrival date:　　Departure date:　　Room number:
Name:　　　　　　　　　　　　　　Job title:
Home address:

　　　　　　　　　　　　　　　　Post code

Telephone:
Company/organisation:
Business address:
　　　　　　　　　　　　　　　　Post code:
Telephone:

Thank you for your time in completing this questionnaire. Should you have an immediate comment or problem please do not hesitate to contact the manager on duty.

Would you be prepared to help us further for a more detailed study if required?

	Yes	No
	☐	☐

In B, we were told that 'there are rigorous quality standards covering customer service and staff training for each of the brands'. Management groups composed of hotel general managers in an area meet regularly to act as quality circles and target on improving certain activities. Quality is measured through complaint statistics and the use of 'mystery guests'.

Again, at C we were informed that 'quality standards are strongly emphasised'. At a formal level, there is a small head office committee composed of two or three hotel general managers and the sales and marketing director which formulates policies. Informally, compliance is enforced by regular visits by head office staff to hotels but no formal measures like repeat business or complaints given from a questionnaire are used.

In D, quality standards in the group are enforced by inspection and a customer complaints procedure from which customer complaints statistics are produced. This kind of inspection is also found in E, where 'the maintenance of centrally negotiated quality standards is crucial to performance measurement'. This is viewed as an operations matter, with the regional managers regularly visiting hotels. To a minor extent internal auditors who appraise the financial controls also have a role. Further monitoring is achieved by a customer comments survey which is pre-addressed to head office covering areas like quality of service, room standards, restaurant and bars, and general comments. The replies are analysed and hotels categorised into one of three grades according to performance.

At F, we were told that 'as well as the quantitative profit target there is considerable stress on meeting qualitative targets in terms of high standards of service, the full development of staff, and conformity to the brand standards'. Interestingly, this was the only company to incorporate these standards into its bonus scheme structure, details of which are given below. These quality standards included a 'quality audit' and a percentage score awarded by a 'mystery guest'.

5.4 Rewards

As we have noted above, 'rewards' can be defined very broadly. In most of our sample, potential penalties were imposed upon managers if they persistently failed to meet budgeted profit targets, although two of our companies (B and D) noted that there were 'no real sanctions' for hotel managers who failed to meet the budget. In some firms (A and E), by contrast, it was quite explicit that managers could either be moved or dismissed for a persistent failure to achieve budgeted targets.

Two-thirds of our sample employed some form of bonus system, with rewards in all cases being based upon budgeted versus actual results. In two firms, C and D, bonuses were not used and their introduction was opposed by the two directors in question, for essentially the same reason: negative experience of the effects of such bonuses. As one of these directors put it, 'managers were more concerned with bonus maximisation than the business of running their hotels'.

Taking the four companies that paid bonuses, the only scheme not based purely on budget versus actual figures was found in F. In this firm, the objective was described as 'to treat the hotel GM [general manager] as an MD [managing director]'. The scheme is based upon 'bottom-line profit after all non-controllable expenses' and involves the payment of a flat percentage of salary if the budget is achieved. Although based upon a final profit figure, allowances can be made for the impact of factors not considered at the time of the budget (for example, a delayed refurbishment programme). Up to twice this percentage can be added for beating the budget. Finally, a similar flat percentage is payable if quality targets are met. These involve achieving a certain threshold score in a 'mystery guest' visit, satisfying a standards audit, and demonstrating the existence of a 'personal action plan' (part of an 'Investors in People' initiative). This type of bonus scheme is now being applied at deputy and departmental manager level.

In A, a banded bonus is paid for achieving 95 per cent of budgeted net profit. The maximum bonus payment is obtained at 115 per cent of budgeted net profit. In the last financial year, just over a quarter of managers had been paid some level of bonus. In B, bonuses were paid based upon the achievement of cash earnings, but bonuses were targeted at specific areas of concern at any given time. For example, the bonus might be targeted at catering cash earnings. In E, a banded bonus is paid for achieving budgeted net profit (after depreciation but before any rental or notional rental charges).

5.5 *Summary*

As the literature suggests, given that hotel investments can essentially be viewed as 'programmed' decisions, in that outcomes can be reasonably predicted from past experience, performance appraisal systems based upon budgeted results are used. There is also considerable similarity in the non-financial performance indicators used.

However, there are real differences in the approach to reward systems. There exists a clear dichotomy, based upon adverse past experience of bonus schemes, between those firms which have schemes based upon budget versus actual profits, and those which do not. While in those firms which do not pay bonuses the budget is seen unambiguously as a forecast of cash and profit flow, where bonuses are paid the budget is sometimes seen primarily as a target, in one case with provision being made against non-achievement. The position is summarised in Table 5.2. There appear to be no obvious contingent factors which explain the differences in attitudes to bonus schemes, or in the use of budgets as targets within those firms that use such schemes.

Table 5.2 Summary of budget preparation and bonus systems

Company	Preparation of budget	Target or forecast?	Bonus system?
A	Iterative	Target	Yes
B	Top-down	Target	Yes
C	Iterative	Forecast	No
D	Bottom-up	Forecast	No
E	Iterative	Forecast	Yes
F	Iterative	Forecast	Yes

6
Investment Appraisal in the Hotel Industry

6.1 Introduction

The archetypal hotel investment may be thought to be described by a construction phase in which negative cash flows occur, followed by a stream of increasing positive revenue cash flows from which cash costs (largely fixed) would have to be met. This would reflect a 'classical' investment pattern which the literature suggests is best appraised by application of the net present value rule. In fact, our interviews revealed that the reality of investment appraisal in the hotel industry is a good deal more complex than is suggested by our archetypal example. In the first place, the types of investment decision tend to be quite varied. Before discussing the results of the interviews and the methodologies used by individual companies, it is worth categorising the types of decisions encountered in our sample.

1. New builds
   1.1 new hotels
   1.2 extensions to existing hotels
   1.3 facility additions (e.g. leisure clubs, gymnasia)
2. Acquisitions of existing hotels
3. Disposals of existing hotels
4. Equity stakes
   4.1 stakes in new hotels
   4.2 stakes in existing hotels
   4.3 stakes involving management contracts[1]
5. Refurbishment programmes

---

1 A management contract is usually a long-term arrangement between the hotel owner and the contractor, where typically the contractor 'brands' the hotel, markets it through its own central reservations office, and supplies the hotel general manager (who then employs the hotel staff at the hotel owner's expense), in exchange for a fee based on a percentage of turnover and/or profit.

Generally, the most simple cash flow patterns are exhibited by 2 and 3, with the most complex arising under 4.3. While the net present value appraisal rule is easily applied to Cases 1 to 3, care is necessary in defining the relevant cash flows in cases 4.1 to 4.3.

The second complication is that of what may variously be described as the terminal, exit, horizon or continuing value of the hotel. Unlike many 'simple' investment projects, such as the purchase of a piece of industrial machinery, a hotel does not usually have a finite life, at least in the short to medium term. To some extent, the problem is similar to that of valuing a company. A discounted cash flow approach to this problem consists of estimating the cash flows for a specific forecast period, typically until a 'steady state' scenario can reasonably be assumed, and adding in the present value of the horizon or continuing value of the firm (*Copeland, Koller and Murrin* (1990), *Gregory* (1992)). As can be shown (e.g. *Keane* (1992), *Gregory* (1992)), in such a steady state,[2] a price-earnings multiple and DCF approach to horizon valuation can be consistent.

As regards the complications caused by investments in categories 4.1 to 4.3, only one firm in our sample was currently actively involved in such projects. None the less, the area may become of increasing importance since, in general, there was a growing interest in the area of management contracts (A and B were among those expressing such an interest). Such contracts are often associated with the contractor taking an equity stake in the hotel. It is also worth noting that in principle the building and operation of a hotel in any firm can be regarded as two distinct investing activities. On the one hand, the purchase of a hotel is a property investment, while the operational side can be viewed as a 'management contract' or service-type activity. A firm *could* choose to invest separately in either side of the business.[3] It would appear that in the literature on property valuation and investment appraisal directed at practising valuers, the use of DCF techniques is widely recommended (e.g. *Brett* (1983), *Morley* (1983a, 1983b)).

---

2 Specifically, when the growth rate, dividend payout ratio, and cost of capital are constant in perpetuity.

3 At the time of writing, one US hotel operator, Marriott Inc., had just separated its businesses into two individual listed companies, reflecting such a division.

6.2 Strategic considerations

It must also be acknowledged that strategic issues such as branding, location and package style (e.g. tour versus business hotel, star ratings, fitness and leisure facilities, etc.) are of fundamental importance. All our sample companies were well aware of this, and appeared to assign more importance to these strategic areas than to the pure numerical analysis. However, the style of the strategic analysis differed along both a formality axis and upon whether or not consultants were employed.

In F, the strategic analysis involved a complex scoring system based upon detailed customer mapping (both in the geographical and demographical senses); they also sometimes employed local consultants to carry out more detailed investigations. At the other end of the spectrum, both A and D relied upon personal inputs (including site visits) by directors before acquisitions were analysed; consultants were employed in neither case, with D being particularly negative with regard to their usefulness. As is described below, this company also had the least formal approach to investment appraisal. In B, most investment decisions tended to be centrally driven, and a feature of this firm was that most 'new build' decisions were strategically determined on a site basis; consultants were not normally used. C had the most diverse range of the decision types described above, and employed a sophisticated four-level analysis (see below); they always employed consultants to prepare a feasibility study before finalising the financial appraisal. E also felt that the 'new build' decision was primarily driven by strategic considerations, and occasionally employed consultants in the analysis stage. This firm also emphasised that even after the financial appraisal had been completed, there was a need to scrutinise all the variables (e.g. room rates, occupancy projections) in the decision, not just the financial indicators of performance.

As regards the initiation of new projects, for the most part 'new builds' were determined by reference to strategic considerations at a senior level within the hotel company. However, in the case of C, consideration of a management contract with an equity stake could also present a reactive consideration of an investment project. Expansions of existing hotels could either be initiated by the hotel manager, or by head office with consultation with the local manager, except in the case of B which tended to be heavily centralised with new projects normally being centrally initiated.

Refurbishments tended to be initiated at both levels, and often in response to a set time pattern.

6.3 A consultant's overview of the investment appraisal process

Given the role played by consultants in the investment appraisal process, as a part of our investigation we interviewed one of the major management consultants in the hotel industry,[4] Pannell Kerr Forster Associates (PKFA). The consultancy that they provide is mainly in the market research and cash flow appraisal stages of new hotel project analysis. A description of their analysis process is given below.

The consultancy becomes involved in feasibility studies on potential new investments initiated primarily by hotel groups. The expertise is needed because of their worldwide knowledge of the hotel industry and their independence when the feasibility study is required as a 'bankable document' if it is necessary to raise funds.

A typical feasibility study takes between four and six weeks. The work commences in the field and focuses on five areas: an economic overview; site evaluation; competitive market supply; the demand for accommodation (the crucial area which usually generates 70 per cent plus of income); and the demand for other facilities. An extension to cover the evaluation of the project, including a financial appraisal, can also be conducted.

The economic overview is based initially on library research to obtain such details as population demography, economic reports including those from banks, interviews in the field with surveyors, planning and tourism authorities, chambers of commerce, economic development units, and so on.

The site evaluation covers: size, topography; nature of area (e.g. greenfield or residential); transport; local amenities, distance to demand draws (e.g. stately homes, conference facilities or sporting venues); distance from commercial and industrial areas; climate; and location of competitors.

---

4 We are grateful to both these firms, Pannell Kerr Forster Associates and Howarth Consulting, for the information provided to assist this research project.

Assessment of the competitive market supply is based on data gleaned from a range of sources, including interviews with local hoteliers, chambers of commerce, local tourist boards, planning departments and others; review of local hotel guides, regional guides, hotel brochures and tariffs of hotels; a review of market reports; discussions with tour operators; and reference to the extensive in-house database. The consultant's database covers 600 hotels (50 per cent in the UK) with occupancy, rate and full profit and loss account details. The information on hotels in the UK is analysed into London and provincial with data provided at city level and by type of hotel, while abroad the data will also distinguish by city and hotel type (e.g. airport). A detailed description of the database profile is given in Table 6.1 overleaf.

The results of this process is data on: (i) total hotel supply analysed by number of hotels, number of rooms, and grade; (ii) potential changes in the supply analysed by hotel and operator, rooms and category, and timescale; and (iii) primary competitive hotel supply with full details of facilities, tariffs including meal costs and conference facilities, nationality mix, market mix, average room rates achieved, occupancies, discounts by market segments and details of major contracts (e.g. with airlines).

Depending on the location, the demand for accommodation may be derived from such sources as corporate; conferences and meetings; tourist and leisure; and airline crew. The sources of information on demand are questionnaires to potential corporate customers, and interviews with conference organisers, convention bureaux, airlines and tourist authorities, among others.

The information collected is input into a series of interlinked spreadsheets analysing current and future market conditions. Projected occupancy is based on the selection of penetration factors of market demand segments and the average rate based upon recommended room rates and room discounts. Detailed projects for up to ten years are derived, including an allowance for assumed inflation. Depending on demand from the client, calculations of cash flows before interest and tax to give IRR and NPV are modelled.

In DCF exercises the discount rate would have regard to the long-term bond yield in the country with the addition of a risk factor in the range 2½ per cent to 6 per cent. As an example, a new build

Table 6.1 Pannell Kerr Forster: profile of database

Monthly surveys	Contributors	Data collected
London	78 hotels	Occupancy and average rate; Food and beverage revenue/cost; Nationality statistics
Provincial UK	300 hotels	Occupancy and average rate; Food and beverage revenue/cost
UK plc	7 groups comprising 366 hotels	Monthly summary P&L account
German	180 hotels	Occupancy and average rate; Food and beverage revenue/cost

Annual surveys	Contributors	Data collected
UK Trends	231 hotels	Annual P&L account by line item
Eurocity	250 luxury hotels in 28 cities	Occupancy and average rate; business and nationality mix; Staffing ratio
Eurotrends	421 hotels in 15 countries	Annual P&L account by line item
Golf Trends	116 golf courses	Key statistics and annual P&L account

may be deemed riskier than an existing hotel and have a higher discount rate based on the investors' perceived risk; beta factors are not considered. Exchange rates in foreign developments can pose a significant problem in less-developed economies such as the former Eastern Bloc countries. The banks provide growth and inflation forecasts but the future remains highly uncertain. The cost per room is a factor only in determining the reasonableness of the outcome for a new build property.

Valuation

The consultancy also carries out valuations. The information-gathering approach is similar to investment appraisal. Valuations are always based on DCF calculations with, in some cases, regard for the multiple of future earnings. In such cases the multiple ranges from 8 to 12 depending on the market and the individual property. This system would not cater for 'trophy' hotels where prices are not earnings based. In some cases, a market-transactions-based approach may be required, although one current problem is the paucity of comparable transactions on which to 'anchor' valuations.[5]

6.4 The financial appeal of hotel investments

The practices employed by individual hotel companies range from the very simple rules of thumb used by D ('the investment must cover its interest cost in the first year, and we take a two- to three-year view of the investment') to a complex analysis of internal rate of return (IRR) on total and equity investment in the case of C. The research found that every major investment appraisal process is in use, together with a few 'home-grown' techniques which are in some cases derivatives of the four standard approaches (payback, accounting rate of return (ARR), IRR, and net present value (NPV)). However, it should also be noted that projected cash flows can sometimes be 'massaged'; as one finance director put it, 'Investment appraisal is painting a picture – there is no point in revealing a position that is too far in advance of the target rate.'

An interesting feature of the analysis is that there is a marked diversity of approaches to the financial appraisal process even

---

5 This problem was noted by the *Financial Times* in connection with the widely differing valuations reported by and in the Queens Moat Houses case.

though the decisions being appraised are relatively homogeneous. At first sight, it is hard to find explanatory or 'contingent' factors which explain this disparity, other than that those firms with centralised group controls and dominant leadership styles (companies A, B and D) tended to use more simplistic approaches.

However, further analysis of D reveals that although it is a part of a multinational conglomerate enterprise, it has only become so relatively recently. In addition, the charismatic head of the hotel company remains in post and has considerable freedom of action; noting this, together with the fact that most investment decisions were made prior to the takeover of the company, leads us to suggest that companies 'rooted' in the hotels and leisure sector tend to have dominant leadership styles associated with centralised control systems and simple rule-of-thumb investment appraisal techniques. By contrast, those with parent companies located outside the hotel and leisure sector tended to make fuller use of DCF techniques. To explore this argument in more detail, a description of the financial analysis employed in each company is given below. A summary table of company characteristics and investment appraisal techniques is given in Table 6.3 on page 89.

Company A

There has been little acquisition or disposal activity, although there have been various extension and refurbishment programmes. All capital investment projects are appraised on a payback basis, although this is not payback as usually defined. Payback is based on *profit* recovery (defined as cash flow less depreciation). There is no standard payback criteria and the profit payback period of the project is but one factor in the decision; however, as an indicator the maximum payback period allowable for extensions is 75 months. This payback calculation is based on the change in estimated future profits generated by the investment rather than changes in cash flows (although in the hotel industry these may be close) since buildings in this company are depreciated at low rates.[6] The estimates of the parameters which will cause the change in profit are generated by the hotel, checked by management accountants for reasonableness, and entered into the planning

---

6 In many firms, buildings are not depreciated at all. Queens Moat Houses had the 'most liberal' policy in the industry, with not even fixtures and fittings being depreciated.

model which estimates quarterly profits. The hotel does not fund the expenditure but depreciation is charged, with rates of around 4 per cent for buildings and 10 per cent or more for refurbishments, and these amounts are taken into account in the payback calculations. Profit changes are also looked at as a direct variable, as are changes in room occupancy rates.

Company B

The company is active in the acquisition and disposal of hotels. The strategy in this area is one of the main responsibilities of senior managers who control the implementation of refurbishment programmes, extensions, acquisitions, and disposals. Acquisitions and disposals are planned and appraised using internal staff, though sometimes with the assistance of consultants. The accounting function provides financial information to assist with these decisions but geographical location and strategic fit of the hotel are the dominant factors in the decision.

Capital expenditure is separated into 'normal' spending (refurbishment, etc.), which is not subject to formal analysis but is carried out according to set programmes agreed with head office, and 'development', which is appraised following a centrally (group level) determined capital budgeting process. Programmes for new development are regarded as strategic decisions which are costed and initiated at group level, with smaller projects (such as hotel extensions and hotel redevelopments) being initiated at the hotels division head office level.

The first stage of the process concerns the strategic decision on location and hotel type (brand); the initiation of the former might be triggered by an event such as the availability of a site. The appraisal then proceeds with a five-year feasibility study covering profitability and cash flows. ARR, payback and IRR all feature, with the main emphasis being upon ARR and post-tax payback. ARR is used as a simple preliminary test, with the first-year return now being set at 5 per cent above the country-specific cost of borrowing. In the case of a 'greenfield' site a break-even position is required in the first year. There are exceptions to this, in that a slower build-up is allowed in the case of strategic moves. A parallel test which must also be satisfied is the payback criterion. This specifies a maximum period of five to seven years based on post-tax cash flows. Although on 'standard builds' an IRR calculation is made using cash flows for the first five years, it fulfils no real decision-making role. Exit or horizon values at the end of the project's life are used in these IRR calculations. The real use of these IRR calculations tends to be in cases where there is phasing of construction or acquisition payments resulting in complex cash flow patterns.

All cash flows are estimated in money (nominal) terms, and analysis of overseas projects is made using local cash flows and local borrowing costs. Sensitivity analysis is carried out on major capital projects. The analysis shows some alternative scenarios to the main feasibility forecasts (e.g. if occupancy is 5 percentage points lower or if average room rate achieved is 5 per cent lower).

Abandonment decisions are initially driven financially. The bottom 20 per cent of hotels by hotel profit contribution (HPC) and cash profits are identified and analysed both geographically and by brand. A disposal list can then be identified, along with the budgeted cash flows of these hotels; however, in order to make a portfolio of hotels saleable, some attractive hotels may be included in a disposal package since 'a portfolio needs to contain some nuggets'.

The company has traditionally approached new investment on a wholly-owned basis but in recent years, in order to break into new markets while still working within sensible capital restraints, several new projects have been set up on a joint venture or management contract basis with outside partners or owners. The underlying appraisal techniques for such projects are essentially the same as for wholly-owned developments in that the underlying hotel operation must be sufficiently profitable; that is, the company would reject a project where the hotel itself was unviable even though the profit share/fee paid to the company gave an acceptable return in isolation.

Company C

Although the majority of hotels are wholly owned, this company does have hotels where it holds a majority or minority equity stake and runs it under a management contract.[7]

Given that the hotel is active in seeking out new opportunities,

---

7 A typical management contract is for 20 to 25 years with an option for a further ten years.

there is a need to assess a range of projects which includes hotel extensions, new hotels (construction and acquisition), and equity stakes. Project initiation comes from two sources: the hotel managers in the case of expansion and refurbishment; and head office development department in the case of new ventures. Given that some of the new ventures involve equity stakes and management contracts, there is a need to appraise not only the viability of the whole project but also a package consisting of revenue to the company from the equity stake and the management contract.

The formal appraisal system is based around an IRR rule, although payback may be used for some minor refurbishment projects. Broadly, specific cash flows (including an inflation element) are forecast to five years after opening, by which time it is felt that the hotel should have reached maturity. The initial cash flows considered mirror the budget statements used by the company, and include assessment of room occupancy, rate, food, beverage and other sales, together with payroll and other cash expenses, yielding the controllable cash flows, from which are deducted management fees, property taxes and insurance, and capital expenditures[8] (typically set at a fixed percentage of turnover). The variables are considered at a site-specific level, and no generalised rules of thumb are employed. At a later stage, if the venture looks viable, consultants are employed to test the assumptions and conduct a feasibility study.

Continuing or horizon value is factored in using a multiple of year five cash flow for the calculation of a five-year IRR. The exercise is repeated for a ten-year horizon, with the same multiple being applied at that time. At this stage, the result is a return on the hotel investment.

The return on the company's stake is then calculated by taking the appropriate share of cash profits, and adding on the management fee income (no head office fixed costs are considered in respect of the latter as it is felt that capacity exists to handle more of these contracts). An IRR is calculated on this stake, with a lower multiple

---

8 These replace the depreciation figure used to estimate profit in any management contract assessment, although as the finance director observed, assuming steady capital expenditure on refurbishment, operating cash flows and profit are closely linked.

of cash earnings being utilised, but with the assumption that the management contract is retained for the duration of the agreed term. Finally, the IRR on the equity stake is considered, for both the hotel as an entity and the company's stake, by deducting interest charges from the present cash flows, and utilising the same 'continuing value' multiples used previously.

Given the complexity of the analysis in C, the investment model pro forma is reproduced as Table 6.2.

In the analysis, it appears that the return on the company's equity is the key indicator; a rule of thumb for an acceptable return is 1.5 times the current corporate borrowing rate, although this can be increased in the case of risky projects. The project has to achieve this return as a minimum, irrespective of its success in meeting the other benchmarks which are employed (see Table 6.2). These include the need for the *hotel's* IRR on equity to be at least equal to the current interest rate. The group regards it as important for the hotel partners to make a fair return in order to avoid any reluctance to maintain and refurbish the hotel to the required standard. In this context, the management fee is negotiable, and can be altered to change the balance of return between partners and the company. Sensitivity analysis (± 5 per cent) is also conducted as part of the appraisal process.

The project hurdle rates are set by the parent company, but the minimum rate can be changed according to circumstances; an example given was that if it were felt that short-term interest rates were temporarily low, the hurdle rate could be increased.

Finally, when submission is made to the parent, additional figures for 'profit with the venture' and 'profit without' are presented. After a full divisional analysis has been carried out, around 10 per cent of projects make it to this stage of the process.

Company D

This company tended not to be involved with 'new build' type projects, although it was involved in expansion through acquisition of single hotels or groups of hotels. Neither DCF nor payback was employed, with the company basing its formal appraisal on an accounting analysis for the first three years after acquisition. The acquisition itself could be driven by strategic fit, or on an

Table 6.2 Investment appraisal pro forma in C

Major assumptions

Total investment £	Inflation %
C share y%	Interest z%
Total equity x%	
Total loan $(1-x)$%	
C equity $(y \times x)$%	
Outstanding value of loan: year 10 £	
Outstanding value of loan: year 5 £	

Project return (note 1)   Year 1   Year 2 etc..
Cash profit before interest
Return on investment %
Internal rate of return: year 5 (%) year 10 (%)

C return (note 2)
Share of cash profits (y%)
Management fees
Total
Return on C investment
Internal rate of return: year 5 (%) year 10 (%)

Return on equity (note 3)
Cash profit before interest
Interest at z%
Cash profit after interest
Return on equity
Internal rate of return: year 5 (%) year 10 (%)

Return on C equity (note 4)
Share of cash profit (y%)
Management fees
Total
Return on equity
Internal rate of return: year 5 (%) year 10 (%)

NOTES:
1 Total project: assumes outright sale. Residual value α times cash profit before interest in year 5 or year 10.
2 C investment: assumes sale retaining n year management contract. Residual value β times cash profit before interest in year 5 or year 10, plus NPV of remaining n years of $(n + 10)$ year management contract.
3 Total equity: IRR based on cash flow after interest and capital repayments. Assumes outright sale. Residual value α times cash profit before interest in year 5 or year 10, less outstanding balance of loan.
4 C equity: IRR based on cash flow after interest and capital repayments. Assumes sale retaining n year management contract. Residual value β times cash profit before interest in year 5 or year 10, plus NPV of remaining n years of $(n + 10)$ year management contract, less balance of loan.

opportunistic basis; in both cases, location was deemed to be the critical factor. An acceptable criterion for investment was for the hotel to cover the interest cost of financing in its first year, and for it to make profits by years two to three. However, for the most part the analysis was informal; not only did the accounting profit requirement need to be met, but following site visits by two key directors both had to 'feel' the investment was correct. If either felt negatively about the project, it was rejected.

Company E

Decisions on new hotel building or acquisition and hotel divestment are driven initially by strategic analysis and are a head office concern; these are often backed by 'gut feel' on the relative value offered by the costs of hotels in different geographical locations. Decisions on extensions and alterations to existing hotels are typically 'joint efforts' between hotel GMs and head office. The key part of the process is the feasibility study, which includes forecasts, a strategic analysis, and estimates of NPV and rates of return.

The financial appraisal is seen as being an important factor in these feasibility studies, but for each case these studies are presented to the board in a manner that allows discussion of all aspects of the investment. Strategic issues are of major concern here. There is no single 'cut-off rate' applied rigidly across all investments, and recognition is given to the fact that some investments (e.g. public health inspectorate recommendations and fire regulation expenditures) are 'defensive' and unavoidable. The appraisal process itself uses a model developed by the parent company for a different industry. The time horizon used is 25 years, with the terminal value normally assumed to be the acquisition/build cost of the hotel, increased by inflation (RPI). The effect is to assume constant real property prices. Refurbishment expenditure is assumed to occur on a seven-year cycle. Inflation is built in to all cash flow estimates at current rates. The corporate model then estimates an NPV, project profitability index (PPI), IRR (with and without consideration of the residual value), and average accounting return on investment (before tax).

In terms of the rates of return required, there is a band of acceptable returns, dependent upon other non-financial aspects of the project. The acceptable rates are set by the parent; the detailed process is not known at hotel company level, but rates are activity-specific and some use is made of divisional betas. All variables in the feasibility study are examined as part of the decision process, including occupancy, room rates and so on. However, the chief accountant was of the opinion that the average accounting rate of return over five years was probably the most significant financial indicator in the analysis. Presentation is seen as being a 'critical success factor' in obtaining approval for the project. Some sensitivity analysis is performed, but this is described as 'very informal' at the moment. Divestment decisions are driven by strategic considerations, but are subject to a similar appraisal process.

The appraisal exercise is communicated separately to the general managers concerned in the case of projects involving a hotel extension or other capital developments like a leisure club. The incremental costs and revenues are identified and adjustments are made for any loss of business that may accrue during the building work. Again, wasting assets are depreciated over seven years. The figures are estimated over five years (including the first year) and a return on investment figure calculated using the five-year average profits. This process is gone through in order to help the general managers understand the full implications and expectations of undertaking the new project.

Company F

The hotel division has plans for controlled expansion through the building of new hotels in order to improve the overall return on capital. Market opportunities for detailed investigation are identified by 'mapping' areas in terms of income groups and comparing them with the profile of existing customers. Provided that sites which meet specific criteria are available, a feasibility study is undertaken to: (i) investigate the site and establish the building costs; (ii) carry out a marketing audit to identify the demand and assess the competition; (iii) build a model which forecasts income and costs over a ten-year period. The model is based on the known cost structure and performance of current hotels and a belief that the strong branding will mean that similar performance can be achieved in any suitable area. Inflation is built into the model, as is an exit value which is based purely on hotel building costs indexed by RPI. Taxation is also considered, including the capital gain arising from the increase in value of the hotel through inflation. The central appraisal technique is the internal rate of return but payback and return on capital (annual profit divided by average net book value over the period) are also calculated as the standard form from the group head office requires it. The internal rate of return must exceed 8 per cent plus a 4 per cent allowance for inflation. This rate is dictated by the group to the division and reflects the group's weighted average cost of capital.

As well as new builds the division undertakes major refurbishments and extensions of existing hotel stock. The opportunities are identified through the close contact between hotel general managers and the division's senior management. Any suitable plans are subject to a feasibility study which includes the identification of the marginal costs and revenues but excludes the abandonment value of the project and any elements of the expenditure which are repairs and renewals rather than capital. The approval process is otherwise identical to new builds. Regular refurbishment and equipment renewal does not go through the same process.

All investment models are subject to sensitivity analysis. Around fourteen factors are investigated, including occupancy rates, room rates, the cost of building, levels of membership of leisure clubs, and food margins.

6.5 *Horizon or exit valuations*

As we have noted above, in all cases where IRR calculations are made for both new hotels (purchased or built) and for extensions, they are executed by including a terminal, horizon or exit value at the end of a specific cash flow forecast period. This ranges from five years in the case of B to twenty-five years in the case of E. In C two analyses are performed, one with an exit value after five years and one at ten years, while in F the exit value is calculated at the end of ten years. The most common approach, used by B, E and F, involved uplifting the purchase price or construction cost of the hotel by the rate of RPI inflation, thus assuming constant asset prices in real terms. The cash flow multiple method which has been used for some time in C corresponds with that suggested in *Recommended Practice for the Valuation of Hotels* (British Association of Hotel Accountants (BAHA), 1993) which was discussed at the BAHA conference in December 1993. Broadly, the valuation process was summarised as 'an exercise in multiplying operating profit by 8.5 and dividing by the number of rooms'. This yielded values of £5,000 per room in 1976, rising to £15,000 in 1982 and just over £50,000 in 1990, although it was noted that two significant industry takeovers had involved prices of over £100,000 per room, examples of the gap between valuation and transaction prices.[9]

These guidelines refer to hotels operated solely or primarily with the objective of making a profit. Such hotels should be valued by reference to both recent or current trading performance and future trading potential. The recommended approaches to valuation are either earnings multiple or DCF based,[10] with other methods used in recent transactions not being normally recommended. The basic objective of this valuation is to show the price at which the hotel or group of hotels being valued is expected to change hands under prevailing market conditions in an open market, assuming the existing use of land, buildings, fixtures and fittings, and including the goodwill attaching to the business.

In establishing this open market value, a DCF analysis of cash flows over a period where these can be forseen with reasonable reliability is preferred; a residual value based upon up to ten times earnings would be included. Note, however, that the DCF valuation method preferred assumes that a *current* valuation is required. In the cases discussed above the objective was the establishment of a horizon value, so that this requirement is the direct equivalent of the residual value referred to in the DCF valuation exercise.

Concerning the recommended discount rate, BAHA note that this must reflect the effects of inflation, the risk-free rate of return and a risk premium reflecting the inherent risk of the industry and investment. This is apparently perceived to be approximately equal to the weighted average cost of capital (WACC) of the investor; this perceived equality is, of course, at variance with the prescription of current corporate finance theory, which would argue that the required rate of return is investment-specific rather than investor-specific.

---

9   It is interesting to note that widely different hotel valuations are currently the subject of some controversy in the case of Queen's Moat Houses.

10 It is well known that, given assumptions of constant estimates for growth, return on new investment and cost of capital, earnings multiple and DCF approaches are mutually compatible; for example, see Gregory (1992).

6.6 Post-audit of investments

All the companies in our survey noted that any cash flow or profit projections used at the appraisal stage are incorporated into the budget for the next year. It was also apparent that in the case of new hotel acquisitions, the individual hotel's results would be clearly and separately identified so that discussion of results could take place at board level if necessary. Beyond this, the formality of post-audit processes ranged from no specific further analysis (D, F) to a complex calculation of achieved ARR based on a year 3 exit value in the case of E .

In A , project post-audits are carried out both by separate analysis and by occurring automatically as the forecast changes in revenues and costs are incorporated in five-year and annual budgets. It was made explicit that 'questions are asked if the profit plan is not met'.

Post-audits are also systematically performed in B, with all free-standing development projects being reported at group board level for the first two years of their lives. Cash and profit flows are reported against those planned in the appraisal process. This type of analysis cannot be carried out for major refurbishment projects as the incremental cash flows cannot be readily identified. Instead, the finance director has developed a formula-driven model which specifies what the hotels should have achieved for a given level of expenditure according to type of investment.

In C, investment decisions are subject to post-implementation audit both by the company and the parent through the internal audit function. By contrast, no formal post-audits are undertaken in D, although, as is noted above, individual hotel reported results are identified at board level.

Company E employs a formal system of post-auditing, with the regular post-investment review of capital projects being an integral part of the investment appraisal process known as 'closing the loop'. For new builds the review is based on a return on investment defined both in terms of cash flow and profits. The former measures the trading performance while the latter includes revaluation movements in order to reflect changes in the wealth of the group. The steady-state position is assumed to be reached after three years. For spend on existing hotels a similar process is followed; however, there is the additional difficulty of then having to isolate the incremental revenues attributable to the expenditure. For example, a leisure/health facility will bring in revenue from members which is easily identifiable, as would be the increase in room rates reflecting this new facility, but it will also bring in a new type of customer with perhaps increases in restaurant and bar revenues. The approach adopted is to attribute all additional revenues to the expenditure and ignore the impact of changes in trading conditions. Again, the appraisal uses the return on investment approach with profit and cash flow measures. A steady state is deemed to be reached after two years in the cases of incremental spend.

In F, at present formal post-investment audits are not carried out but the budgets set would clearly reflect the target performance included in the investment appraisal exercise, and individual results are reported at board level.

There appear to be no factors which readily determine the presence of a formal post-audit. It is associated neither with the complexity of appraisal system, nor with the degree of control centralisation. Perhaps the real explanation for its presence is simply an increasing use of post-audit techniques. Four of our sample of six used a post-audit, and the suggestion was that a fifth (F) was thinking of doing so. This increasing tendency to use post-audit would be compatible with that observed elsewhere (*Mills and Kennedy*, 1993). It is also noticeable that four out of six companies using post-auditing is considerably higher than the 48 per cent overall and 40 per cent distribution and hotel industry usage reported by Neale (1989). However, the Neale study was concerned with post-*completion* auditing, a concept of limited usefulness in the hotel industry, where long-lived investments are the norm. Indeed, the only way the concept can be operationalised (except in cases of liquidated hotel investments) is by the inclusion of an assumed exit value, as was practised in E.

6.7 Summary

From our case studies, we can establish no link between size of company and appraisal method used. However, it does appear that the more 'sophisticated' analyses, both in terms of cash flow modelling and employment of DCF techniques, tend to be used by companies which are subsidiaries of non-hotel but non-conglomerate parent firms. In these firms the hotel activity was in some way complementary to the main business, and the parent had a tradition of DCF analysis. However, it should be noted that in the case of C some hotel industry specific model changes had been made to accommodate the complexities of management contracts and equity stakes.

It was also apparent that the least formal investment appraisal processes were found in firms managed in a hands-on fashion by strong characters. By contrast, formal systems tended to be employed where the control systems were such that parent board approval was necessary to go ahead with the project (B, C, E and F). In the other two cases formal board approval was not necessary as the managing director made the decision himself directly (a summary of the investment appraisal techniques used compared with company characteristics is shown in Table 6.3, p. 89). One aspect of obtaining board approval was what might be described as 'sticking to the rules'. Two quotes from our interviewees best sum this up: one explained how there was a need to have a consultant's feasibility study to present as 'a bankable document'; another stated that in obtaining board approval 'presentation is key'.

A further interesting observation is the response which a questionnaire survey would have elicited. Four of our sample (B, C, E, and F) apparently use payback, ARR and DCF methods, yet the emphasis they place on each result shows great cross-sectional variation between firms. Typically, some of these approaches are mechanically gone through simply because they are required by head office, or the group's financial appraisal model automatically produces the result. None the less, this may help to explain findings from recent empirical research that more than 40 per cent of companies use three or more approaches to investment appraisal *(Sangster,* 1993). Another point is that questionnaire surveys may not discover the same richness of technical diversity that case studies can reveal. For example, A clearly stated that they used payback; only further questioning and a look at the models employed disclosed that in fact a profit payback measure was the heuristic rather than cash flow payback. This reaffirms the arguments in favour of case study analyses *(Scapens* 1991); our finding that there is a potential difference between response to questionnaires and actual practical use of techniques mirrors those of *Rickwood et al.* (1987) discussed in Scapens.

It is also the case that in the hotel industry, the decision to be made is typically fairly standard within companies, with a considerable bank of past experience to draw upon. Thus standard rules of thumb such as 'build cost per room' for a given star rating, and expected room yields can be successfully employed; as one finance director observed, 'we are confident we can run hotels profitably provided we can accurately forecast occupancy rates and average room rates'; thus, these areas became focal points in the investment appraisal process. Related to this, we might also observe that in this industry we found no examples of either mutually exclusive project choices or unusual cash flow patterns. Thus, the 'textbook' arguments for favouring NPV against IRR may not have particular relevance to the hotel sector, and therefore the fact that IRR is easier to communicate to non-financial managers may explain why NPV appears not to have been used in any of the cases which we investigated.

Finally, in those companies which did employ DCF decision rules (or ARRs) there was no consistency with regard to the method of discount rate (rate of return) estimation. Although, in general, the acceptable rate was determined by head office, the methods of determination ranged across borrowing rate plus basis points (B) or plus a percentage (C), and head office set rates possibly determined using betas (E, but note that the basis for arriving at betas or the discount rate was unclear) to a head office rate based upon the *group* weighted average cost of capital. However, perhaps such diversity of practice is not surprising, given the different approaches suggested in the theoretical literature. For example, there are alternative equilibrium risk pricing models (e.g. the capital asset pricing model (CAPM), an extended version of the CAPM or a multi-index model based upon the arbitrage pricing theory (APT)) and different theories on the tax shield value of debt (for a summary of the arguments, see *Strong and Appleyard* (1992)). None the less, if we use the average beta of the hotel and catering sector as reported by the September 1993 *London Business School Risk Measurement Service*, and assume that the risk-free rate can be viewed as either around the 3 per cent implied by the current level of the stockmarket,[11] or the 6 per cent implied by the long-run real return on gilts compared with equities (*Barclays de Zoete Wedd Equity Gilt Study*, 1992), the rates looked for by our case companies are not

---

11 At the time of writing, the dividend yield on the FT All-Share Index is just over 4 per cent; if one assumes a real long-term dividend growth rate of 2.5 per cent p.a.

incompatible with those suggested by, say, a CAPM approach to weighted average cost of capital assuming an 'active' debt management policy (*Miles and Ezzell* (1980), *Strong and Appleyard* (1992)).

---

and applies the standard dividend growth model:

$$(\text{price} = (\text{last dividend} \times (1 + \text{growth}))/(\text{return} - \text{growth})$$

and solves for return, the result is that the implicit future real return on the market is around 6.7 per cent. Given a real yield on long index-linked gilts of approximately 3.5 per cent, the current risk premium on equities is around 3.2 per cent.

Table 6.3 Summary of investment appraisal techniques and company characteristics

Company	Industry of parent	Parent mgmt style	Hands-on approach?	Investment appraisal technique	IRR use?	Cost of capital*	Horizon valuation*
A	Hotel & Leisure	Centralised	Yes	Profit payback	No	N.A.	N.A.
B	Hotel & Leisure	Centralised	No	ARR/Payback	Partly	Loan rate +	Cost + inflation
C	Travel	Decentralised	No	IRR	Yes	1.5 × loan rate	Cashflow multiple
D	Conglomerate	Decentralised	Yes	Cover interest (Yr 1) profit (Yr 2)	No	N.A.	N.A.
E	Brewing	Decentralised	No	ARR/IRR	Yes	Business spec.	Cost + inflation
F	Brewing	Decentralised	No	IRR	Yes	Corp. WACC	Cost + inflation

* Companies using ARR or IRR only

7
Conclusion

7.1 *Introduction*

Fitzgerald et al. (1990) identified three different generic service types (professional service; mass service; and service shop), based on comparing the volume of customers processed by a typical unit per day against six other classification dimensions: people/equipment focus; front/back office focus; product/process focus; level of customisation of the service to any one customer; discretion available to front office staff; and contact time available by front office staff. Hotels were classified as service shops which hold the middle ground between professional services, which are high-contact organisations with a customised service, and mass services, which involve limited contact time and little customisation. In service shops, there is a moderate degree of customer contact, customisation, volumes of customers and staff discretion, and the service is provided by a mix of front and back office activities, people and equipment, and of products and processes.

Fitzgerald et al. (1990) indicated that the following features might be anticipated in management accounting systems which produced information for performance measurement:

(i) focus on the performance of competitors;
(ii) emphasis on relative cost structure
(iii) low cost traceability;
(iv) cost collection based on the functional activities of the organisation with use of activity-based costing;
(v) costs not routinely used for pricing decisions.

7.2 *Strategic management accounting*

A focus on the performance of competitors and relative cost structures would be reflected in the use of strategic management accounting. The cases show that the accounting function in hotel groups has considerable involvement in strategic management accounting. The interviewees consistently identified two main strategic management accounting areas:

(i) the provision of information, which includes market and competitor data, that assisted in the development of long-term strategic plans; *and*

(ii) monitoring the market, competitors' price structures and competitors' costs in the short run.

Strategic planning was formalised through the preparation of long-term budgets for durations of three to five years forward. The main objectives were to:

(i) enable management to consider the future;
(ii) explore the effect of alternative strategies and scenarios;
(iii) provide an indication of the future shape of the business; *and*
(iv) highlight the future financial structure of the group and identify and schedule future financing requirements.

The monitoring of the market and competitors was facilitated by the open nature of the industry and the availability of price and some cost data. In the hotel industry, it is difficult for companies to be secretive about prices or costs. With respect to prices, rack rates and other standard terms are publicised and it is possible to pose as a customer to ascertain discounts off the published rates. On the cost side, major components of costs may be determined with a degree of accuracy either by the company or through consultants who publish comparative data. All but two of the cases monitored the cost structures and pricing policies of competitors, typically through an analysis of data obtained from consultants' reports, published financial statements, brokers' reports, and analysts' reports.

7.3 *Management accounting information for costing*

The costing systems were found to be based on marginal costs, but often little effort was put into identifying all marginal costs since margins were extremely high and there was an overriding objective to maximise sales. This finding is consistent with the observation of *Fitzgerald et al.* (1990) that there would be low cost traceability. A further finding that was consistent with Fitzgerald et al. was that all the hotel groups adopted a departmental approach to the collection of costs and revenues, and that the departments were based on the functional activities of hotels. The only inconsistency with Fitzgerald et al. that was found related to a uniform failure to use activity-based costing. The reasons given for this included the integrated nature of the activities, the high margins on most business lines, and the market-based nature of pricing. All other aspects of the costing system were consistent with theory. For example, there was a separation of overhead costs into controllable and uncontrollable categories, and head office costs, with the exception of levies for marketing and training in some hotels, were not charged to individual hotels.

7.4 Management accounting information for pricing

Pricing was a complex area, given the bundled nature of the services provided by a hotel and the distinct market segments in a hotel. In all the case studies pricing policy was essentially market driven along the lines suggested by pricing theory, and management accounting had little to contribute to the pricing decision (a finding that is wholly consistent with the observations of *Fitzgerald et al.* (1990) that costs would not be routinely used for pricing decisions). The main source of variation between the case studies was in the degree of central control exercised over the pricing policy of individual hotels. Typically, promotion and bargain break prices were determined centrally as was, in the majority of instances, discounting policy. However, hotel general managers had a greater input into the determination of rack rates.

The stated thrust of pricing policy was to maximise revenue as direct costs are low, especially for letting rooms, and fixed costs high. All the accountancy functions concentrated on balancing the occupancy percentage with the average room rate (bearing in mind the impact of occupancy rates on other income from sources like food and beverages) in order to maximise revenue.

7.5 *Management accounting for planning and control*

As was anticipated from a review of *Parkinson* (1993) and *Thornfield* (1991), considerable time and effort was expended by accounting staff and hotel and head office management in drawing up and agreeing budgets. The budgets fulfilled several roles, which included authorisation for the hotel general manager to incur various overhead costs; forecasting and planning both in the shorter and longer term; acting as a channel of communication and co-ordination, especially in hotels which were reliant on the head office for a high proportion of business; motivating staff in at least some of the hotels; a means of performance evaluation and control; and a basis for decision-making.

The budgeting process typically involved two interlinked activities: the long-term budget which covered from three to five years forward, and the annual budget covering twelve months or thirteen four-week periods.

The long-term budgets were updated annually on a rolling basis within the annual budget cycle so that the first year of the long-term budget equated with the annual budget for the following year. There was general agreement among the interviewees that certainly beyond two years forward the figures were very speculative, but it was still felt that the exercise was worthwhile especially for planning financing requirements, which by their nature involve long-term planning, and examining the future shape of the group.

The annual budgets were typically fixed iteratively, with examples of approaches that could be classified as bottom up and top down. The balance of power in this process often reflected the balance of business derived from head office as opposed to being generated locally. Typically, head office would supply the individual hotels with economic and marketing data and a standard pro forma usually in a computer form (for example, on a spreadsheet) for completion. The various meetings between the hotel general manager and senior management would take place before a final version was agreed. The process made full use of information technology, with budget frameworks being issued as standard spreadsheet packages on a diskette or electronically. In general, the budgets were not flexed to reflect actual levels of activity, and variances were purely based on the difference between the budget and actual for each budget line.

There was variation among the cases as to whether the budget was a target, a forecast, or a combination of both. In general, the budgets were intended to reflect a realistic performance target which it was expected that hotels could meet, and therefore were both a target and a forecast of the expected outcome. Outside this formal budgeting system, most of the interviewees also prepared forecasts to estimate the actual outcome for the accounting period and to provide realistic future targets.

Most variation in the approach to budgeting arose from three sources: first, pressures applied by any parent company on the hotel group to provide information; second, the extent to which business is generated locally as opposed to deriving from head office marketing activities; and third, the extent to which budgets are associated with performance evaluation and performance-related rewards.

7.6 *Performance evaluation*

In all the case studies, we found that the performance appraisal system was based upon a comparison of actual and budgeted results. Many of the non-financial performance indicators used are similar across companies. Despite the fact that hotel general managers can influence the capital base of their hotels, only one company used a direct measure of return on capital employed. As was noted, this measure was a sophisticated one reflecting not only hotel profitability but also the holding gains or losses on the hotel. However, the absence of ROCE-type measures should not cause concern if, as was the case in all our companies, planned cash flows from new investments are compared with achieved cash flows. This was certainly so in the year following the investment, since the budget reflected planned cash flows on all new capital investments. As *Tomkins* (1973) demonstrates, this is equivalent to calculating residual income based upon the economic value of the asset acquired, which is in fact a superior appraisal method (in economic terms) to ROCE in any event.[1]

---

1 Although it should be noted that for Tomkins' proof to hold, the cash flows planned at the time the investment decision was made need to form the basis of each subsequent year's budgeted cash flows in respect of the investment. See Gregory (1988) for a more detailed explanation.

Although there are distinct similarities in the approach to the financial and non-financial measures of performance, there is a clear dichotomy in the use of bonus systems. This appears to derive from differing past experiences of bonus schemes, with the result that four of our case studies have schemes based upon budget versus actual profits, while two cases firmly rejected such schemes. In both those companies, the interviewee expressed the view that in his experience bonus schemes promoted short-termism. It was also noted that in those firms the budget is seen principally as a forecast of cash and profit flow, with the emphasis being placed on accurate forecasting.

In those firms where bonuses are paid the budget is sometimes seen primarily as a target, in one case with provisions being made against non-achievement, and sometimes as a forecast. There appear to be no obvious factors which explain these differences in the use of bonuses, or in whether or not the budget is seen as a target or a forecast in those firms which use bonus systems. One interesting observation is that in only one case study company was a quality standard actively incorporated into the bonus system.

7.7 *Investment appraisal*

We noted that the types of decision necessitating an investment appraisal included new builds, acquisitions, extensions, expansions into leisure clubs and other activities, divestments, management contracts and equity stakes. Although some of these decision alternatives were not found in all hotels (for example, the majority did not take equity stakes or undertake management contracts) there is none the less a good deal of commonality between the decisions faced in each of our case study companies. It might therefore be postulated that such a situation would be expected to give rise to similar approaches to investment appraisal. The surprising finding of our research is that there is, in fact, a wide disparity in the methods of analysis used. Evidence of the use of all major investment appraisal methods was found, with the preferred main methods ranging from a profit payback, to accounting rate of return (both using a simple return on initial investment and a more sophisticated method which included holding gains on hotels) to discounted cash flow methods. In addition, one company used a method based upon covering the interest charges on the borrowing necessary to finance the purchase of a hotel.

We also noted that in most firms there was a considerable bank of past experience to draw upon, and to some extent this allows for the use of standard rules of thumb such as 'build cost per room' for a given star rating and expected room yields. These sorts of rules tended to serve as checks and balances in the investment appraisal process. Another factor which possibly influences method choice is that we found no examples of either mutually exclusive project choices or unusual cash flow patterns. The 'textbook' arguments for favouring NPV against IRR depend largely upon the presence of these factors, and their absence, together with the fact that IRR is easier to communicate to non-financial managers than NPV, may explain why IRR is universally preferred to NPV in all those cases where a DCF method is employed.

We also found no evidence of any link between size of company and appraisal method used, but found that the more 'sophisticated' analyses, both in terms of cash flow modelling and employment of DCF techniques, tended to be used by companies which are subsidiaries of non-hotel parent firms which are not conglomerates. In these firms the parent had a tradition of DCF analysis. It was also the case that, where the complex cash flow patterns associated with such matters as staged payments and equity stakes were encountered, IRR was the preferred appraisal method.

We also noted that there was an association between management style and appraisal method. The least formal investment appraisal processes were found in firms managed in a hands-on fashion by strong characters; in these companies the managing director personally took the investment decision. Formal systems tended to be employed where the control systems were such that parent board approval was necessary to go ahead with the project . We also noted that in the latter companies the process itself, together with the documentation it produced, could perhaps be interpreted as evidence of having followed a 'due diligence' procedure.

Where DCF or ARR decision rules were used a variety of approaches was adopted in arriving at a suitable discount rate. Although this was determined by head office, the methods of estimation included borrowing rate plus basis points, borrowing rate plus a percentage, a head office rate set and believed to incorporate a hotel-specific beta, and a head office rate based upon the *group* weighted average cost of capital. Perhaps such diversity of practice is not surprising, given the different approaches suggested in the theoretical literature and that, using the average beta of the hotel and catering sector together with a risk premium of between 3 per cent and 6 per cent, the rates used in the case companies were not incompatible with those suggested by a CAPM approach to weighted average cost of capital, assuming an 'active' debt management policy.

In conclusion, although many of the investment appraisal approaches used in practice were not those recommended by the literature, in over half the cases investigated the net result is that the methods used may be regarded as producing broadly similar decisions to those which would have resulted from the application of 'textbook' methods.

7.8 Some observations on possible future developments in management accounting practices of hotel groups

During the course of discussions with the interviewees, some broad indications of the trend of developments in their management accounting systems were discerned.

Strategic management accounting

The highly competitive nature of the industry and the problems experienced by a number of hotel groups during the economic downturn of the early 1990s will mean that the role of strategic management accounting in providing information for long-term planning and ascertaining the group's relative competitiveness will become increasingly important.

Costing and pricing

There was little evidence of discontent with existing costing practices which generally highlight contribution at a departmental level. None of those interviewed had any plans to adopt activity-based costing and few had given the matter any thought. In all the cases a prime objective of management was the control of labour costs to ensure that these varied with the level of activity. Some of the case study companies had sought to achieve this through altering conditions of service and employing part-time staff. To meet this priority, management accounting systems will continue to focus more tightly upon labour costs and their relationship with activity. Prices will remain driven almost entirely by market forces and it seems unlikely that management accounting information will be greatly involved in this area.

Control

Budgeting will continue to be the key element in controlling individual hotels in a group. Computer links and the advent of spreadsheet and financial modelling software has greatly improved the ability of the management accountant to explore a range of scenarios, iterate the budgeting process, and report and follow up variances. In essence the process has changed little, and no dramatic changes were anticipated by the case study companies; however, it is possible that there will be more emphasis on longer-term budgets, especially as regards the financial structure of the group in an effort to avoid financial difficulties.

Performance evaluation

As regards the performance evaluation of hotel managers, it seems likely that the emphasis on budget versus actual performance will continue. On theoretical grounds, in so far as the budget reflects planned investment cash flows (as they seem to in our case study companies), this is compatible with discounted cash flow based investment appraisal rules. Reliance on comparisons of budgeted and actual performance can also be defended on risk-sharing grounds, as in the agency theory literature. It may be the case that performance evaluation becomes more widely based, with increasing emphasis on non-financial indicators, including, in particular, measures of quality. Equally, it may be that there could be a switch to a more aggressive use of budget information, for example involving bonuses based upon budget versus actual profits at departmental levels within hotels. If this occurred, there could arise the attendant danger of short-termism on the part of managers.

It seems unlikely that there will be much change in the usage or non-usage of bonus schemes in general, however. As we have noted, corporate management appears to be either strongly in favour or strongly against the use of bonus payments, based primarily upon the personal past experience and preferences of certain key individuals. We would be surprised if any of our sample firms switched policy on the employment of such schemes, as long as the current senior management remains in post. However, in those firms which do use bonuses, we would expect to see the level at which the payments are made to be pushed down within some hotel chains.

We might also expect to see greater use of DCF techniques in the performance evaluation of hotels as opposed to hotel managers. On theoretical grounds, present value of future cash flows versus current disposal value would appear to form a rational basis, as it has the merit of being forward-looking. However, the position is complicated by the presence of abandonment and postponement options, which could theoretically be appraised using option pricing models *(Stark,* 1990).

Investment appraisal

We would expect to see the increasing use of discounted cash flow methods, partly promoted by the more complex cash flow patterns associated with management contracts and equity stakeholding which may be growing trends. The BAHA valuation guidelines, which recommend the use of DCF techniques, may also be influential here. It may also be the case that hotel companies more actively explore the splitting of the service provision and property investment sides of the business. However, as we noted in Chapter 6, the hotel industry is one where simple decision heuristics may be of considerable use. If hotel groups remain in the 'traditional' business of building or purchasing hotels and letting rooms, managers may prefer to stay with these simple rules of thumb. None the less, changing environments concerning interest rates, investment risk premiums and inflation rates may force a reappraisal of some of these rules. At present, only one of our sample companies used a 'sophisticated' method for establishing the discount rate. If there occurs a growing awareness of risk pricing models in the industry, we may see greater use of beta factors in the setting of hotel project discount rates.

References

Arnold, J and Hope, A (1990), *Accounting for Management Decisions*, (2nd edn.), Prentice Hall, Hemel Hempstead.

Bhattacharya, K (1988), 'A Management Accountant's Role in SWOT Analysis', *Management Accounting*, February, 66, 2.

Bloom, R, Elgers, P and Murray, D (1984), 'Functional Fixation in Product Pricing: A Comparison of Individuals and Groups', *Accounting, Organisations and Society*, 9, 1.

Brett, M (1983), 'Analytical Investment Techniques' in Darlow, C (ed.), *Valuation and Investment Appraisal*, The Estates Gazette Ltd, London.

British Association of Hotel Accountants (1993), *Recommended Practice for the Valuation of Hotels*, BAHA, London.

Bromwich, M (1990), 'The Case for Strategic Management Accounting: The Role of Accounting Information for Strategy in Competitive Markets', *Accounting, Organisations and Society*, 15, 1/2.

Bromwich, M and Bhimani, A (1989), *Management Accounting: Evolution not Revolution*, CIMA, London.

Chartered Institute of Management Accountants (1982; revised edn. 1991), *Management Accounting: Official Terminology*, CIMA, London.

Copeland, T E, Koller, T and Murrin J (1990), *Valuation: measuring and managing the value of companies*, Wiley, Chichester.

Davis, E W, Coates, J, Collier, P and Longden, S (1991), *Currency Risk Management in Multinational Companies*, Prentice Hall/ICAEW, London.

Diesing, P (1972), *Patterns of Discovery in the Social Sciences*, Routledge and Kegan Paul, London.

Dorward, N (1987), *The Pricing Decision: Economic Theory and Business Practice*, Harper & Row, London.

Edey, H C (1966), *Business Budgets and Accounts*, (3rd edn.), Hutchinson, London.

Edwards, J, Kay, J and Mayer, C (1987), *The Economic Analysis of Accounting Profitability*, Clarendon Press, Oxford.

Emmanuel, C, Otley, D and Merchant, K (1990), *Accounting for Management Control*, Chapman & Hall, London.

Everett, M D (1989), 'Managerial Accounting Systems: A Decision-Making Tool', *Cornell Hotel and Restaurant Administration Quarterly*, 30, 1.

Fitzgerald, L, Johnston, R, Brignall, S, Silvestro, R and Voss, C (1990), *Performance Measurement in Service Businesses*, CIMA, London.

Galloway, D and Waldron, D (1988), 'Throughput Accounting: The Need for a New Language for Manufacture', *Management Accounting*, 63, 10.

Goldberg, S M, Green, P E, and Wind, Y (1984), 'Conjoint Analysis of Price Premiums for Hotel Amenities', *Journal of Business*, 57.

Gregory, A (1987), 'Divisional Performance Measurement with Divisions as Lessees of Head Office Assets', *Accounting and Business Research*,17, 67.

Gregory, A (1988), 'A Review of Divisional Manager Performance Evaluation', *Management Accounting*, January.

Gregory, (1992), *Valuing Companies*, Woodhead Faulkner, Cambridge.

Harrison, L and Johnson, K (1992), *UK Hotel Groups Directory 1992/93*, Cassell, London.

Hofstede, G H (1968), *The Game of Budgetary Control*, Tavistock Institute.

Holland, J (1993), 'Bank–Corporate Relations: Change Issues in the International Enterprise', *Accounting and Business Research*, 23, 91.

HMSO (1969), *A Standard System of Hotel Accounting*, London.

Hotel Association of New York City (1986), *Uniform System of Accounts for Hotels*, (8th edn.), New York.

Kaplan, R S (1984), *The Case for Case Studies in Management Accounting Research*, paper presented at the American Accounting Association Annual Conference.

Kaplan, R S (1986), 'The Role for Empirical Research in Management Accounting', *Accounting, Organisations and Society*, 11, 4/5.

Keane, S M (1992), A Survey of the Valuation Practices of Professional Accounting Firms, ICAS.

Miles, J A and Ezzell J R (1980), 'The Weighted Average Cost of Capital, Perfect Capital Markets and Project Life: A Clarification', *Journal of Finance and Quantitative Analysis*, September.

Miles, J A and Ezzell J R (1983), 'Capital Project Analysis and the Debt Transaction Plan', *Journal of Finance Research*, Spring.

Mills, R W and Kennedy, A (1993), 'Post-completion auditing in practice', *Management Accounting*, October.

Mills, R W and Sweeting, C (1988), *Pricing Decisions in Practice: How are they made in UK Service and Manufacturing Companies?*, CIMA Occasional Paper, CIMA, London.

Mohr, L G (1985), 'The Reliability of the Case Study as a Source of Information', in Coulam, R and Smith, R (eds.), *Advances in Information Processing in Organisations*, 2, JAI Press, London.

Morley, S (1993a), 'Investment Valuations' in Darlow, C (ed.), *Valuation and Investment Appraisal*, The Estates Gazette Ltd, London.

Morley, S (1993b), 'Investment Valuations' in Darlow, C (ed.), *Valuation and Investment Appraisal*, The Estates Gazette Ltd, London.

Neale, C W (1989), 'Post Auditing Practices by UK Firms: Aims, Benefits and Shortcomings', *British Accounting Review*, 21, 4.

Parkinson, G (1993), *Hotel Accounts and their Audit*, Institute of Chartered Accountants in England and Wales, London.

Reece, J S and Cool, W R (1978) 'Measuring Investment Centre Performance', *Harvard Business Review*, May/June.

Rickwood, C, Coates, J B and Stacy, R (1987), 'Managed Costs and the Capture of Information', *Accounting and Business Research*, 17, 68.

Ryan, R, Scapens, R W and Theobald, M (1992), *Research Method and Methodology in Finance and Accounting*, Academic Press, London.

Scapens, R W (1990), 'Researching management accounting practice: the role of case study methods', *British Accounting Review*, 23, 3.

Stark, A W (1990), 'Irreversibility and the Capital Budgeting Process', *Management Accounting Research*, 1, 3.

Strong, N C and Appleyard, T R (1992), 'Investment Appraisal, Taxes and the Security Market Line', *Journal of Business Finance and Accounting*, 19, 1.

Thomas, A L (1974), 'The Allocation Problem: Part Two', in *Studies in Accounting Research No. 9*, American Accounting Association.

Tomkins, C (1973), *Financial Planning in Divisionalised Companies*, Haymarket, London.

Thornfield, A (1991), *Accounting in Hotels* (3rd edn.), CIMA, London.

Wijeysinghe, B S (1993), 'Breakeven Occupancy for a Hotel Operation', *Management Accounting*, 68, 2.

Zimmerman, J L (1979), 'The Costs and Benefits of Cost Allocations', *The Accounting Review*, July.